"I SELL EXPERIENCES. ALL KINDS OF EXPERI-ENCES. SEXUAL EXPERIENCES ARE JUST PART OF IT. YOU PUT ON THE 'TRODES AND YOU GET TO KNOW WHAT IT FEELS LIKE TO RIDE WITH A GANG, OR GET IN A BAR FIGHT, OR WALK AROUND IN DRAG, OR DO A THOUSAND-DOLLAR-NIGHT CALL GIRL, OR SOME SHANKY TEENAGE HOOKER OR A WEST HOLLYWOOD BOY HUSTLER. WHAT-EVER YOU WANT . . ."

Lenny Nero can supply you with other people's kicks—if you have the cold cash to pay for them.

Brace yourself.

You may think it's safer than reality.

It's not. Not when you get in over your head.

STRANGE
DAYS

JAMES CAMERON is the award-winning writer and director of *The Terminator, Terminator 2: Judgment Day, The Abyss, True Lies,* and *Aliens.*

STRANGE DAYS

JAMES CAMERON

twentieth century fox presents a lightstorm entertainment production a kathryn bigelow film ralph fiennes angela bassett strange days
juliette lewis tom sizemore michael wincott vincent d'onofrio music by graeme revell music supervisor randy gerston
additional score by deep forest costume designer ellen mirojnick edited by howard smith, a.c.e. production designer lilly kilvert
director of photography matthew f. leonetti, a.s.c. special visual effects by digital domain executive producers rae sanchini lawrence kasanoff
story by james cameron screenplay by james cameron and jay cocks
produced by james cameron and steven-charles jaffe directed by kathryn bigelow

DOLBY
IN SELECTED THEATRES

Soundtrack available on LIGHTSTORM/EPIC SOUNDTRAX

A PLUME BOOK

PLUME
Published by the Penguin Group
Penguin Books USA Inc., 375 Hudson Street,
New York, New York 10014, U.S.A.
Penguin Books Ltd, 27 Wrights Lane,
London W8 5TZ, England
Penguin Books Australia Ltd, Ringwood,
Victoria, Australia
Penguin Books Canada Ltd, 10 Alcorn Avenue,
Toronto, Ontario, Canada M4V 3B2
Penguin Books (N.Z.) Ltd, 182-190 Wairau Road,
Auckland 10, New Zealand

Penguin Books Ltd, Registered Offices:
Harmondsworth, Middlesex, England

First published by Plume, an imprint of Dutton Signet,
a division of Penguin Books USA Inc.

First Printing, October, 1995
10 9 8 7 6 5 4 3 2 1

 REGISTERED TRADEMARK—MARCA REGISTRADA

ISBN 0-452-27581-4
CIP data is available.

Printed in the United States of America
Set in Century Expanded
Designed by Stanley S. Drate/Folio Graphics Co., Inc.

Welcome to My Nightmare

I've been to the South Pole, flown barrel rolls in a supersonic jet fighter, and been to the bottom of the ocean in a submersible, but the most terrifying thing I've ever faced is the blank page.

At the beginning of any writing project is the agonizing period in which nebulous ideas dance before the mind's eye like memories of a dream, and vaporous vague shapes take on human form and begin to answer to their names. By the end of it there is Sarah, or Ripley, or Lenny, and it is almost impossible to remember a time when they did not exist in my life.

I find the writing follows a logarithmic curve. Plotted against time, the curve is almost flat at first, then curves upward until it is nearly vertical. Almost nothing happens for a long time. I daydream, I read books, look at movies, trying to get in the mood. Trying to will a world into existence. I circle around it, nibbling at the edges, writing notes about the social infrastructure and expounding to no one in particular about the themes of the thing, like I'm writing a book report.

Then slowly a change happens. Without warning, it becomes easier to write a scene than to write notes about the scene. I start sticking words in the mouths of characters who are still mannequins, forcing them to move and to walk like animated corpses in a George Romero film so they can hit the milestones of the plot. Slowly their movements become more human, and their skin gets pink with the flow of blood.

The curve inflects upward, the pace increases. The characters begin to say things in their own words. By the end of this period I'm writing ten pages a day. The last day becomes endless, often stretching round the clock to the following noon. The last thirty pages of *Terminator 2: Judgment Day* were written in one thirty-two-hour sprint. *Strange Days* was the same. The curve becomes almost vertical as the thing seems to come alive. I become a witness only, a court reporter getting it down as fast as I can.

Lenny Nero was born in 1985 when I decided to write a film noir thriller taking place on New Year's Eve 1999. I was fascinated by the dramatic and thematic potentials of the millennium, and the idea of doomsday as a backdrop for the redemption of one individual. It was conceived as pure film noir, with a tech edge, hence the main character's name: Nero means "black" in Italian, my favorite language. At that time I made a few notes, totaling less than five handwritten pages. In this preliminary sketch, the story consisted of a street hustler, a loser named Lenny Nero, who is squired around the urban decay of future L.A. by an unwilling limo driver, a woman named "Mace" Mason. He is a black-market buyer and seller of human experience, recorded and played back directly into the brain, and he enters a dance of death with a psychotic killer, who seems to be homing in relentlessly on Lenny's ex-girlfriend, Faith, whom Lenny has difficulty protecting because she won't have anything to do with him. I called it "The Magic Man," because Lenny can get you anything . . . like magic. I never got around to writing it, at least not that decade.

The remarkable thing, when I look at those pathetic handwritten scrawls now, is how the basic template of the story never changed, despite the long odyssey of getting from those notes to a shooting script in 1994.

Sometime in late 1992 I pitched this idea to Kathryn Bigelow. It had lain dormant all those years as one of those things that I knew I would get around to sooner or later but never did. I began to worry that if I waited too long, the millennium would no longer be far enough off to be science fiction. So with two directing projects looming in front of me (*True Lies* and *Spiderman*) which would take me into the mid-nineties, I decided to let another director take over a piece that was near and dear to me.

Kathryn, with her edgy visual style, was the obvious choice. We had worked together as producer and director previously on *Point Break,* which she directed while I (ghost) wrote and executive-produced. We made a good complementary team, and I knew her as an insightful, gifted filmmaker who was also tremendously responsible. Her previous four films had been done on budget and on schedule, which few filmmakers can claim, least of all me. In addition, she is that avia raris in mainstream filmmaking—a director who cares deeply about the characters while approaching the material with an intensely visual style.

Fortunately Kathryn liked the pitch and turned down her other offers, agreeing to sit and wait while I wrote the script. Now the pressure was on. The problem was I had never written anything remotely this densely plotted and character driven. I circled and circled the computer, like a dog slinking around trying to work up the courage to steal food from a sleeping drunk.

I couldn't crack the plot to save my life. Kathryn had added her own spin to the piece, opening up the story and giving it thematic weight by having the murder tapes lead inexorably to an explosive incident involving the LAPD and a potential race riot of biblical proportions.

This concept fit well with my idea for a mega-party that teeters on the edge of complete social collapse, but it was proving very snaky trying to integrate it with the film noir erotic-thriller love story. Too many notes, as the Emperor said.

Kathryn waited months with diminishing patience while I pondered and pondered. I wanted Elmore Leonard to come to me like Elvis comes to Christian Slater in *True Romance* and tell me how to do this shit. Finally, one dark night in January 1993 I got the breakthrough I needed and the piece started to flow. Following the accelerating curve described above, the "scriptment" was written in about a three-week period, ending in a two-day marathon frenzy.

Eight years of vague ideas, three months of intense pondering, four weeks of writing and a few days of jamming . . . and what emerged was this kind of two-headed calf that was neither a treatment nor a script. I had gone up a hill and come down a mountain . . . intending to write a forty-page treatment and winding up with a document 131 pages long. Somewhere in the middle of the war Lenny and Mace and Faith came alive and it was just easier to write what they said than to describe it in outline form. Any scenes that I couldn't crack right away, I skimmed over and used the novelistic treatment form to sort of mumble through.

So what you have in your hands is at once a kind of pathetic document; it is as long as a script, but messy and undisciplined, full of cheats and glossed-over sections. But it is also an interesting snapshot of formatting a moment in the creative process. It contains notes and references and textures that do not exist in the finished script. It takes the time to gaze around at a grim future world and paint it in neon colors . . . it gets in the mood first, then tells the story.

It is also, possibly, of interest to fans of the film to see the evolution of ideas. When I was unable, because of my commitment to *True Lies,* to do the actual first draft screenplay, I hired Jay Cocks to come in and kick it into shape. Between Jay and Kathryn, ideas flew like crazy—visualize whirled peas. Their restructuring of my unwieldy piece was efficient and focused, while retaining the style of the meandering, quirky dialogue. They wrote it down to a manageable length and shaped it to Kathryn's vision. Though Jay and I did very little writing together, we are both proud of the collaboration. It was the way it is supposed to be, and so rarely is.

Jay merged the two clubs, Mondo 2000 (named for the cyber-punk magazine) and Retinal Fetish, and collapsed together the scenes for efficiency, without losing a single beat.

Kathryn and Jay pushed for a confrontation that would test Mace and Lenny's friendship, and came up with the idea in which the tape becomes the focus of a crisis between them, with Lenny wanting to use it to save Faith while Mace demands that he do the right thing and bring Jeriko's killers to justice. Lenny passes Mace's test, and is redeemed in that moment, allowing their relationship to continue and, by the end, grow. This was a pivotal moment that is completely missing from the "scriptment," and I think you can see how important that is in the film.

So what you are about to read is a flawed document, a work in progress, a detailed study for a painting. But what is remarkable to me when I reread this, is how parts of it have stood up through the entire process with barely a single word changed, while other parts are almost unrecognizable in the final film.

Some names got changed: Tick, the lowlife from the opening scene, got merged with Tran the Vietnamese gang-banger wirehead. Constance became "Vita" Minh in the final draft; Kathryn took the name from Tran's girlfriend, who got the axe in the second draft. Burden Spreg, the original name of the bad street cop, became Burton Steckler and has been changed throughout this document as well, apparently because the studio found out that the former was a real guy's name—pure coincidence, but why upset somebody?

The value of this "scriptment" lies solely in it being presented unchanged, unedited, unpolished. It is the first hurling of paint against the wall in the visualization of a future world and the people in it.

Enjoy. Meanwhile, I have to write another one . . . so it's back to slinking around that sleeping drunk.

STRANGE DAYS

1:06 AM, December 30, 1999

Blackness.
We hear:

VOICE

Ready?

SECOND VOICE

Yeah. Boot it.

It starts with a burst of bright white static exploding across the darkness. A high singing whine on the audio track gives way to street sounds and rapid breathing.

An image wavers and stabilizes: the inside of a car, seen from the backseat in POV.

A *nervous* POV. We're in the car, sitting in the backseat, and we're nervous, the view swinging around, showing the street rolling by outside the windows, then whipping back to the two guys in the front seat. These are not happy well-adjusted men. They're hyperventilating and red-eyed like a couple of lab rats in an electroshock experiment. They want the cheese so bad they can taste it but you just know they're going to get their little pink paws fried.

The driver is a Hispanic guy named "SPAZ" DIAZ. The guy riding shotgun is a white guy, LANE, who looks very strung out. Couple of crackheads. The car, from what we can see, is a mid-seventies barge, piebald with primer.

They are talking almost nonstop, cranked up and tense. Lane pulls a pantyhose over his head, smearing his features into a pig-like mask. He hands one back to us.

Our POV looks down, into the pantyhose, which comes up over our field of view.
We realize: this is not some ride-along verité video.
WE ARE ONE OF THESE GUYS. Real honest-to-God point of view, with no cuts, no music. This is not film, it is human experience.

Now the three of us are arguing over who should have which gun. We hear OUR VOICE whining about the 12 gauge.
Lane turns DIRECTLY TO THE LENS, pissed off.

>   LANE
> Lewis, you pussy. You don't want the pump, you
> don't have to use the pump. You want the nine
> millimeter?

>   LEWIS (OUR VOICE)
> Uh uh. I never get to use the magnum. Spaz al-
> ways uses it.

>   LANE
> Well Spaz is stayin' in the car, so you want to
> use the .44 you can use it. Gimme that thing!

Lane snatches the shotgun from us and hands over a big stainless steel revolver. Our hand takes it. The POV looks down as our shaky hands snap open the cylinder, check the rounds, snap it closed.

>   LANE
> Buncha fuckin' women. Okay, pull in up here.
> The alley, right he— THIS FUCKING ALLEY!

We rock forward as Spaz brakes suddenly. He curses in Spanish and backs up, then turns into an alley. The head-lights illuminate overflowing dumpsters, trash every-where. Lane tells Spaz to take it slow. Then he points to an open door up ahead. There it is.

A Chicano in a filthy busboy uniform comes out the door, which is an island of light in the dark alley, carrying pro-duce trays heaped with garbage. He glances over his shoulder at the headlights as he heads for the nearest dumpster. The busboy goes back inside, his arms full of trays and unable to close the door.
Lane says let's go and we are on the move.
Out of the car, quickly, our own breathing loud in our ears. We even hear our own heartbeat, racing now.
Through the door, after Lane, moving fast.
Into the kitchen. Bright fluorescent glare. The busboy turning, surprised, Lane putting the shotgun in his face. Freezing him. Lane puts a finger to his lips: "quiet" in any language.
We (Lewis) show the magnum to the COOK . . . a young Thai man, thin as a whippet.
We get them down on the greasy floor, Lane controlling them with the shotgun. He looks at us, snaps his eyes toward the front room of the restaurant. We hear voices as we approach the swing door.
Go through.
Whip pan left, then right. Scoping the layout.
Low-rent Thai place. Red wallpaper.
Middle-aged Thai man, the OWNER, by the cash-regis-ter, counting money and writing out his deposit slips. Young Thai WAITRESS, straightening up. The place is empty of customers, as planned. The doors locked.
The owner and the waitress look up, stunned, as we put the gun on them. We hear our voice shouting "Don't move! Keep your hands where I can see 'em!" etc.

Controlling the situation. POV is whipping around, from the front door to the owner to the kitchen where Lane is standing in the doorway covering the cook and busboy, back to the owner as he steps back from the cash register.

With one hand we scoop up the big wad of bills. POV looking at it. Seven, eight hundred bucks in tens and fives.

Now shouting, herding the owner and the terrified waitress into the kitchen, the owner chirping rapidly in singsongy Thai. Telling the girl to be calm and do what they say.

Lane shouting at him to shut up.

Into the walk-in cooler with them. Four scared pairs of eyes as the steel door closes. POV looking around, scanning for something. Sees silverware in the dish-rack and our hand pulls out a spoon, drops the spoon handle through the hole in the cooler door-latch.

Locking them in.

Lane heading out the back door. Laughing, as he looks at the wad of cash our hand is waving in front of him.

We follow Lane to the car. Snap a look down the alley one way, then the other.

Shit! Cop Black-and-White pulling into the far end of the alley.

Heartbeat goes tripletime. Scrambling into the car.

Lane yelling something about a silent alarm.

Door not even closed and Spaz has it in reverse, burning rubber as he launches back down the alley.

SCRRUNCH! The car grinds along one wall as Spaz steers wildly backward. Sparks right next to us. Then—

KBOOM! as we slam backwards into a dumpster and push it right out into the street.

The cop has his lights and siren on and is roaring at us as Spaz cranks the wheel and punches it down the street.

We hear the engine roaring.

Spaz cursing in English and Spanish as he weaves between cars. We pull off the stocking to see better.

Looking back. The cop surges onto the street behind us.

Looking ahead. A red light. Cars stopped, blocking the way.

Cutting to the right, onto the sidewalk, around the cars, into the intersection.

A near miss with cross traffic, then accelerating.

Another red light ahead.

Lane yelling don't stop!

Truck entering the intersection. Everyone yelling.

Spaz cuts the wheel but too late . . .

Clipping the truck and spinning.

The street outside smearing past like the view from a Tilt-a-Whirl.

Then KBLAM! Hitting something, God-knows-what, and launching up and over, and—

KRUNCH! Crushing metal and an explosion of broken glass.

It gets quiet and still.

Tinkling glass as Lane moves.

A beat. Then Spaz is screaming. We see the car is upside down.

Crawling out the side window. A frenzy now.

Whip pan to see the cops pulling up.

Then whipping back to the wreck.

The engine is burning. Flames spreading rapidly.

Spaz inside, pinned, upside down.

Screaming. Blood pumping across his face.

Our hands pulling Lane out.

He comes up running.

We run after him . . .

Sprinting toward the welcoming darkness of an alley.

Panting breath and heartbeats and sirens and somebody yelling.

Gunshots. Looking back. Cops next to their car, firing.
Ahead. Lane running into shadow.
Then a door opening, a man coming out of a metal
firedoor.
Lane grabbing him, throwing him out of the way, hold-
ing the door open as we dive through into—
A stairwell. Lane sprinting up, two steps at a time. Metal
stairs clanging.
Trying the door at the second floor landing. Locked. Shit.
Running up. Dizzying whirl as we run, up and up.

The POV is finally broken by a CUT TO: A man in extreme
closeup, just seeing his eyes and mouth. The eyes are closed,
the eyeballs tracking under the lids, like he is watching a
movie in there.
This is LENNY.

> **LENNY**
> This is great . . . the doors are all locked. Who are
> these losers? Friends a yours?

BACK TO POV as we reach the fifth floor landing. Lane
is coming unglued as he finds this door locked. He
pounds it in frustration. We look down, see cops coming
two floors below. One cranks off a couple rounds at us
and we snap back from the railing.
Pounding up the last flight.
Finally! The door is unlocked.
Blasting through it, behind Lane, onto the roof.
Running all out past AC units and pipes, air vents.
Looking up: an LAPD helicopter orbiting close.
It flicks the xenon onto us and we are running in a vi-
brating circle of blue daylight.
Running along the edge of the roof. Looking down.
Car burning upside down in the street below. The gas
tank explodes, filling the street with orange light.
We don't slow. We're running all out.

Wow . . . the gas tank is a nice touch. Oh, oh, end a
the line, boys.

Ahead, in POV we see the edge of the roof coming up.
Beyond it is another building, about ten feet lower and
separated by a 20-foot alley.
But Lane doesn't slow down. He leaps out across the void
and makes it to the other building, landing in a sprawl.
We reach the edge and look down. Six stories. No ladders
or fire-escapes.
Whip to behind us. Cops running across the roof.
Lane yelling, "Come on, Lewis! Fucking jump, man!"

The POV backs up from the edge and then runs toward
it . . .
Out into the void.
Holy shit . . . airborne. Then—
WHAM! Right in the parapet wall.
Slipping down. Brick wall right in our face.
Looking up . . . bloody fingers holding onto a rusty piece
of pipe running along the edge.
Looking down . . . feet dangling over a 60-foot drop.
A cat walking through a patch of light in the alley below,
oblivious.
Breathing rough and raspy, desperate grunts.
Snapping a look up as the pipe is giving way.
A keening whine coming from us as we scramble to
climb up but—
The pipe wrenches loose and—
Snapping a look down—
Walls rushing past, sound of wind, and our own raspy
scream—
Ground rushing up—
Split-second impression of a cat, looking up, yowling and
running out of the way as—

Pavement fills frame.
A burst of violent red light. Sound like a gunshot . . . but
no echo.
Only silence. And blackness.

CUT TO Lenny. We see a little more. He has something on
his head. Something that looks like a mutated set of Walkman headphones, except they have little gecko fingers that
fit along the temples and over the forehead. Playback trodes.
Lenny whips off the trodes, his eyes snapping open.
He is suddenly gasping for breath, like he got gunpunched.
And his upbeat mood has changed.

> **LENNY**
> What the fuck is this?! Goddammit! You know I
> don't deal in snuff. Christ. How many times I hafta
> tell you?

Lenny is with a guy named TODD COYLE, though everybody on the street calls him "TICK." Tick is a pale-skinned
creature of the night. Long greasy hair, T-shirt and leather
jacket. Some cheap tattoos. Not a class act.

> **TICK**
> Don't have a fucking coronary. I just thought you
> might be interested, is all.

> **LENNY**
> You could've at least warned me. I just hate the
> zap . . . you know, when they die. It just brings
> down your whole day. Jeez, Tick.

> **TICK**
> Sorry.

LENNY NERO is low thirties. Handsome. Charming. And

somehow you want to check to see if you still have your ring
after you shake with him. He is wearing an expensive Italian
jacket, and what he thinks of as a "power tie."
His Rolex isn't real. His greasy hair is too long and curls
around his collar. He needs to shave. There is an aura of
sleaze around him. Like a car salesman. Or a junior agent.
But he has energy, this guy, and plenty of streetsmarts.

They are in a deserted underground parking garage, lit by
miles of fluorescents. Lenny is sitting on the hood of his '97
BMW 1035i. Tick is facing him, sitting in the back door of
his beat-to-shit 70's van. There are a lot of tapes and tech
stuff piled inside the van.

Lenny has a Haliburton case often next to him, like a drug
dealer. In fact the whole setup looks like a drug deal, but it's
not. Though it is illegal. The case holds Lenny's personal
playback deck, his trodes, and a rack of the little tapes in
which he deals. They are about the size of DAT tapes, and
hold about 30 minutes of sensory experience . . . everything
a person sees, hears, and feels . . . recorded directly from
the cerebral cortex at the moment it is happening.

> **LENNY**
> How'd you get the tape? Why didn't the cops put it
> in evidence?

> **TICK**
> Fuckin' moron cops didn't even know the guy was
> wearin'. I guess his head kinda, uh . . . popped . . .
> when he hit, and with all the blood they didn't see
> the rig. Maybe he had it under a wig or something.

> **LENNY**
> Yeah, but how'd it get to you?

TICK

I got ways, Lenny, I got ways. S'why you like me so much, right?

LENNY

(patiently) That's right, Tick. That's why I like you so much.

TICK

Okay, I got a deal with some a the paramedics and one a them found the rig on the way in, you know, workin' on the guy. Paged me and I picked it up down at the morgue. Hadda give 'im five hundred for the record-deck, even though it was pretty banged up. He didn't have a playback-deck so he didn't know what was on the tape. Whadda moron. This piece a tape's worth more than the deck. Right? I mean, it's gotta be worth at least a grand.

LENNY

Tick. Not to dash your hopes, but I don't deal this kinda product, you know that. I'll give you four for it, cause I've gotta cut off the last bit. And my customers don't like edits. They want uncut.

TICK

Fuck that. The last part is the best. You dry-dive six stories and whammo—check-out time. Jackin' into the Big Black, baby. The great beyond. That's what people want to see, and you know it, so don't be doggin' me.

LENNY

Look, I just don't deal it. *No black-jack clips.* It's policy. Got it? Sell it to somebody else.

TICK

You think I can't? I know lotsa people.

LENNY

Whatever.

TICK

Come on, Lenny. I got expenses. I gotta get this
rig fixed . . . look at it, man . . . the blood's all inside,
on the chips and everything.

Tick holds up a Ziploc bag containing a Walkman-sized
stainless steel CORTICAL RESONANCE RECORDER,
or record deck, with a wire running to the SQUID ARRAY,
a matrix of sensors designed to conform to the human head
(this looks much more complex than the playback trodes).
The whole works are covered with congealed blood. The surgical tape which held the recorder to the wearer's body is
still plastered to it. Some chest hairs are still stuck to the
surgical tape.

*SQUID stands for Superconducting QUantum Interference
Device, but more on this later.*

TICK

Gimme six at least. Come on, man, it's the *master*.
This ain't no stepped-on copy. You know you can
make ten dupes and move 'em all.
This's a good clip, here. You were sayin' so yourself
while you were playin' back. Gets you pumpin'.

LENNY

Yeah, well, the first part's okay. Better'n the usual
soaps you bring me.

TICK

Now that is cold, Lenny. I always bring you choice.

Lenny fishes around in a cardboard box at Tick's feet, pulling out a tape.

> **LENNY**
> Yeah, like this low-grade shit here, some girl in a
> fight with her boyfriend . . . it's a test-pattern.
> Nothing happens. I'm snorin'.

> **TICK**
> Hey, you're always saying, "Bring me real life.
> Bring me street life. And, like, one man's mundane
> and desperate existence is another man's Techni-
> color."

> **LENNY**
> I said that? Look, I'll take it for five, and you'll
> make out okay, because in this case it's pure
> cream, you don't have to cut anything back to the
> wearer, which I know for a fact.

> **TICK**
> Ha! That's for fucking sure.

> **LENNY**
> Okay. What else you got?

CUT TO:

Next we see Lenny on the move, driving through the streets
of LA in his BMW. The streetlights and neon flare across
the windshield in a calligraphy of light.

It is seven years from now. Things look pretty much the
same. The newer cars are smaller, more cab-forward, but
they look like cars. The people on the streets aren't wearing

silver lamé jumpsuits. Clothes look like clothes. No radical
new styles.

The economy is worse. The jobless rate is up. New housing
is down. All the indicators are creeping steadily into the red,
as they have for most of our lives. California, the Shake 'n
Bake state, is still mailing out IOU's and waiting for the Big
One to make Barstow into beachfront property.

The freeways are a nightmare of gridlock, with smaller cars
packed closer and closer together. Gas is over three bucks a
gallon. Unemployment and inflation are way up. Real estate
agents have the highest suicide rate in the country. The
Mexicans are going back to Mexico, because it's not looking
so bad anymore.

The visible changes are not radical but incremental. More
gang graffiti, more homeless wandering the streets, more
businesses closed, more burned-out buildings. Racial and
class tensions are higher than ever. The city seems constantly on the verge of chaos and martial law, a legacy of
social dysfunction which has grown steadily worse since the
eighties. Pressure seems to be building for an upheaval
which will dwarf the Spring Riots of '92. The city is wound
tight.
The future . . . tense.

But people still go to work, to movies, to restaurants. It's
business as usual in the big city.

The really big changes are all behind the scenes, in high
technology, in telecommunications, in the way it's all wired
up. And the average guy is barely aware of these changes.
They seep into his consciousness as the new toys hit the con-
sumer market and the new technologies become part of life.
The way things like lap-top computers and cellular phones
go from novelties to basics in two or three years.

The technology that Lenny deals in is still illegal.
Developed in the mid-nineties, the CORTICAL RE-
CORDER was created for surveillance applications and
used by the intelligence community, initially. Use of these
"SQUID RIGS" quickly spread to the FBI, DEA, Treasury
Department, and other Federal law enforcement agencies,
for use in undercover and sting operations, replacing the old
audio-only "body wire."

The "headwire" turns the "wearer" into a human video cam-
era, providing images and sounds directly from the eyes and
ears of the undercover agent. In the last couple of years it
has trickled down to widespread use in urban police depart-
ments, and has been approved for psychologists to use in
therapy.

The courts argued over the admissibility of cortical recordings as evidence. But it was decided that they were more
reliable than video and audio recordings, since advances in
digital technology have made it easy to alter video images
and sounds undetectably. So far the technology does not
exist to manipulate or falsify the cortical recordings. They
can be copied, with a significant loss of quality, but basically
what you see is what happened.

Lenny has the radio on. The KXXX's talk radio host is hyp-
ing a big blow-out street-party which will happen tomorrow
night . . . New Year's Eve. They're closing down six square
blocks downtown, by the Bonaventure Hotel, to celebrate
the city's transition into the new millenium. It'll be like
Mardi Gras, with food, music, dancing and general madness.
Talk radio host calls it the party of the century.

Because this is 1999.
And tomorrow night, Friday night, December 31st, will be
the last night of the twentieth century.

The next day the date will be January 1, 2000.
The Big 2K.
Out with the last thousand years, in with the next.
Civilization will lurch into its third millenium.
The start of the Trillenium, you could call it.

There is a strange hysteria pervading the city, and most of
the Western world, as the new year approaches. A mixture
of jubilation and dread. All the religious cranks have come
out of the woodwork, claiming the advent of the Last Days,
the Apocalypse, with various forms of the death and destruc-
tion to arrive at midnight, when the calendar rolls around to
the year 2000.

Thousands have gathered in the desert for a Rapture, having sold or given away their worldly possessions. There is a
madness upon the land. People chant on the streetcorners.
There are threats of war worldwide, famines and natural di-
sasters.
Wars and rumors of wars.
Any given moment in history always seems to fit the Biblical
description of the Last Days so it's not hard for the zealots
to get everyone whipped up.

It's hard to distinguish the particular millenial madness
from the day to day madness of street-life in LA seven years
from now.
Riots are a common occurrence. Drive-by shootings are so
prevalent that in some areas the dead sometimes lie in the
street unattended. Choppers circle constantly. Fires burn
here and there almost all the time. You can drive past whole
streets and neighborhoods devastated by violence. In places
it looks like Beirut. But of course, life goes on. Kids play
among the ruins.

Civic leaders are overwhelmed. Their social and economic

recovery programs aren't working. As the millenium approaches, they feel more and more like they are just re-arranging deck chairs on the Titanic.

Cops are tough, and less interested than ever in civil, or even human rights. Lenny's kind of crime is the least of their worries. He inhabits a kind of gray zone anyway, invading people's privacy certainly, but the laws are unclear about the new technology and as long as he keeps a low profile the cops stay off his ass.

The history of the nineties in LA and most urban areas is the history of the decline of the infrastructure. By 1999 private security has replaced the police in most affluent areas as the protective membrane against crime. A condom against the virus of violence.

There has been a proliferation of private security services, patrols, bodyguards, and computerized alarm systems. There are computerized car alarms and even personal (portable) digital alarm systems, carried in a purse or coat pocket, which are tied into a digital cellular network. Hit a button and your distress signal pops up on a screen, showing location, and nature of threat, if you have time to enter it . . . allowing the security service to dispatch an armed response unit.

It has become common for middle-income people to use security drivers, driving taxi-like armored cars, to get around . . . especially at night. Security is the biggest growth industry in LA, and all urban areas in the US.

The court system is collapsing under the weight of rampant street crime, cops are understaffed and underfunded, frustrated and mean, alienated from the communities they protect. They have become like US soldiers in Vietnam, unable to tell the enemy from the populace they are there to defend.

Private security protects only those able to pay.
Obviously these services are not available to the poor. They are on their own, like always. Safety is no longer the right of all citizens, but a luxury for the haves.
The have-nots are worse off than ever.

If you want to sum up the history of the next seven years: things got bad for a while.
Then, they got worse.

As parts of LA burn, the rich party on in Beverly Hills and Bel Air, and the upper-middle-class burghers huddle in their newly gated communities in the hills of Encino and Calabasas.
More and more expensive neighborhoods are retreating behind steel gates. Setting up their own guarded perimeters, and patrols.

And everyone watches and is watched.
LAPD Aerospatiale helicopters circle, looking down with their infared cameras. There are crime-prevention cameras on many streetcorners, to extend the visual reach of the police.

There are security cameras in malls, cameras in office buildings, cameras in banks, cameras in schools, cameras in convenience stores, even citizen patrols with handycams. The cops use handycams, fighting fire with fire, when they shake somebody down on the street . . . because nobody, including the courts, trusts their word anymore. And there is a rise in drive-by shootings of people walking with cameras, and action news cameramen . . . as if the gangs are putting out a message: no pictures. The social battles of the video age are fought with images, not guns.

Reality shows and amateur video shows dominate TV programming.
It is the age of scopophilia, voyeurism, and vicarious living. The mania for amateur porn, starting in the early nineties, has steadily increased.

We like to watch. It is a surveillance culture.

Lenny, we will come to find out, is an ex-cop. He worked the street in uniform for the requisite minimum, but his talent for hustling and role-playing quickly landed him a job in Vice. He found himself attracted to the surveillance assignments, and worked closely with the electronic surveillance team.

Lenny wanted out of Vice so he slid into the surveillance team, doing "wire" work and bugging for Narco, Homicide, etc. He couldn't stand Vice anymore . . . all that jumping out of closets with a tape recorder the second the girl asks for the money, busting crack addict hookers, the weird scenes with S and M, B and D, getting dragged daily through the gutter of human sexual dysfunction.

Surveillance team took him into a new realm, snooping on people's private lives, getting inside their heads. It appealed to his basically voyeuristic nature . . . he found he liked it, and had a talent for it.

That's where he first saw the "squids." He learned to "wire" himself and others with concealed squid rigs, taping the recorders to the small of his back, or under the balls, and covering the squid array with wigs, hairpieces, baseball caps.

Something happened on a big narcotics sting that he doesn't like to talk about. He left the LAPD under a cloud, and has been a civilian for almost two years.

He now inhabits a social sphere composed primarily of street hustlers whose primary motivation is survival . . . hookers, druggies, post-punk criminal outsiders, anarchists, black marketeers and assorted high-tech lowlife: hackers, cyberpunks, wireheads and input junkies.

But with a little charm and a well-chosen wardrobe, he also accesses the social strata on which he feeds . . . the rich. At parties, at nightclubs, he curries a select clientele to whom he sells his illicit wares . . . bootleg experiences, slices of other people's lives, vicarious thrills for the jaded and insu-lated elite.

He is to them what the coke dealer was in the early eighties. A backdoor friend. A tolerated sleazebag, who somehow con-noted a kind of dangerous hipness by his presence.

Lenny is on his cellular, setting up a meeting later with a client. Some doctor. Lenny says he has to make a stop first, then he'll come by the guy's house. He makes another call to somebody, promising to pay them what he owes after the first of the year, things are crazy right now.

Lenny is an operator. A fast-talking salesman, scam artist. Hustler. A dealer. He is a creature of the moment. Not a planner. To him the city is like a big coral reef . . . a big food chain. Alive and dynamic. A place where a fast fish can eat and avoid being eaten.

Lenny's great gift is insight into human nature. He twists it and uses it to manipulate people and situations, but it is a great and rare talent. Because it is a compassionate insight. The talent of a world-class psychiatrist or bartender or hooker—the ability to see into people, to say to them what they may not even be able to say to themselves.

He knows about longing and desire, pain and frustration. He knows what people want, what their subconscious minds want, and why they do things. He knows the importance of fantasy and of seeing through other eyes. To him it is not scopophilic, or voyeuristic, but a search for understanding, enlightenment, knowledge. This is the serious side of him, the side he hides with humor, the side that fuels his scams and is simultaneously the key to his redemption.
The talent made him good at his job as a Vice dick, but ultimately he saw the total hypocrisy of his work. He was good at something he couldn't stand doing.

He couldn't be a Vice cop anymore because he couldn't make the bad guys be bad guys in his head anymore . . . couldn't do his job.
He just saw a lot of people wanting something out of the one life they got, something which worked for them, even though it may not have been the panacea of missionary heterosexual sex which mainstream "surface" culture prescribed, even though it may be a path which caused them pain and humiliation.
Christlike, in a strange way, he understands all, forgives all.

Lenny driving gives us a snapshot of the exact moment in history the story is taking place . . . the date, the time, the city, and the energy building to the New Year.
We see Christmas lights still up.
Santa Clauses on the lamp-posts in Beverly Hills.
We hear the talk radio host giving us a manic connection to the world we know now.
This is not some wild Bladerunner future, but our future.
The future we're going to be living in all too soon.
Outside the windows we see street-life . . . and in the dis-

tance, fires lighting the sky. The chirping radio keeps the dread of the impending Apocalypse at bay.

CUT TO:

A woman's feet moving along the steel rail of a train track at night. The woman has no shoes, and her stockings are ripped, her feet half bare. Red painted toenails almost black in the cold light from distant mercury-vapor lights.

IRIS runs along the track, stepping off once in a while as she loses her balance. She clutches one shoe pointlessly to her chest.
She is swearing and crying. The latter has run her heavy mascara, leaving two tragic streaks down her pale face. Despite this we see that she is attractive, though her dress and make-up seem designed to convey overt sexiness. Her white skin is complemented by a wild mane of curly red hair.

She is in her early twenties, and the harshness of her life has just begun to harden her features. Especially around the eyes.
On top of this is layered the terror of the present moment.
She looks lost and without hope, in fear of her life.
Her breath comes in hitching sobs, and her eyes are wild like those of a wounded deer.

She runs through a train yard, between the cold steel walls of freight cars, looking behind her frequently. As if she is being pursued. Her breath hangs cold in the December air, and she hugs herself in her thin dress, clutching her single high-heel under her arm.

Behind her, in the sky, a police helicopter is circling. Its xenon beam plays over the train yard, sweeping over the cars. She hunches into the shadows of a freight-car as the beam passes over. Looking under the cars she sees an LAPD patrol car cruising down a street adjoining the yard, its searchlight sweeping toward her. It moves on.

She continues her run, moving away from the direction of the patrol car. She runs down an embankment in the dark, gravel hurting her feet, and climbs through bushes which slash at her.

Her run becomes a frenzy.

She reaches a chain-link fence. Crying, she scrambles over it, cutting her hands and ripping her dress.

Another patrol car passes two blocks away.

She crouches in the tall grass until it rounds a corner out of sight.

Iris sprints down an alley between buildings. Rats run over cardboard boxes of garbage, scattering into the shadows ahead of her. She doesn't seem to notice. All she cares about are the lights, the police lights, and the sound of the helicopter droning, circling.

She pauses at the mouth of the alley, scanning the well-lit street beyond. There are people here, though they are mostly downtown low-life street people.

Across the road and up a half-block is a brightly lit sign marking the entrance to a Red-Line subway station.

She walks along the sidewalk toward the sign.

It is like a sanctuary. She keeps her eyes off the sign, feeling exposed as she walks openly, her heart pounding. She is a mess, but in this section of town people barely glance at her.

LOW ANGLE on her bare feet, standing out amid the shoes and boots of winter.

SHE CROSSES the street, and reaches the sidewalk just as

a Black-and-White rounds the corner at the end of the block, behind her.

IN THE CRUISER are TWO COPS, who are scanning the street.
They look intense. Revved up.
They are BURTON STECKLER, a massive, barrel-chested street-lifer in his mid-forties, and DWAYNE ENGELMAN, an aggressive hard-on in his twenties with a brush cut, a Nautilus body, and a face like a ferret.

She's a hooker, Engelman says. *Vice'll have her in the book. We can pick her up later.*
No, Steckler replies. Now.
His eyes are cold as he scans the pedestrians.

IRIS knows the cops are behind her. She is terrified to turn.
Finally she can't stand it any more.
She breaks into a run.
The patrol car speeds up suddenly, roaring after her.
Iris sprints along in her bare feet, all-out like a track runner.
The Black-and-White screeches to the curb next to her.
The doors fly open and the two cops jump out.

Iris hits the stairs down to the subway station at a full-tilt boogie, knocking down some poor old guy whose groceries go flying.
She trips on the landing, spins sprawling across the filthy tile floor, and comes up running.
Panting with fear and exertion she clears the turnstyles like a hurdler.
The cops pound down the stairs two at a time.
Steckler draws his 9mm. In his eyes we see an unaccountable craziness . . . the feral gleam of a hunter who has as much at stake somehow as the prey.

Street people fall back as Steckler thunders through them. They aren't about to get in the way of this juggernaut cop and his boy wonder.

The two cops reach the platform.
No Iris in sight.

MOVING WITH THEM as they slow to a walk, scanning. A couple of low-lifes standing around, waiting for trains, eye them warily.
Step back.

Engelman gets a call on his Rover, asking if they need back-up.
He says they have lost the suspect, and inexplicably gives the description as a black male. Tells the dispatcher every-thing is fine.

A train pulls into the station with a woosh of air.
The few people board. The platform is empty.
There is only the sound of the cops' footsteps as they move along.
With a pneumatic hiss the train's doors begin to close.

Suddenly Iris breaks from behind a column up ahead at a full sprint. Steckler unleashes his size 13 cop shoes, thunder-ing along the platform to intercept her.

Engelman has straight-armed his pistol, yelling FREEZE! which of course she has no intention of doing.

Iris clears the doors just as they hiss shut, forcing herself through.

Her momentum carries her clear across the car, where she slams into the far wail and staggers back, almost falling.

She gasps for breath and looks up to see Steckler crash against the outside of the doors she just came through.

The train starts to move.

Steckler tries to force the doors apart . . . can't.

He aims his gun through the window.

Thinking fast Iris dives to his side of the car and presses herself up against the solid wall next to the door, where he can't see her.

OUTSIDE, Steckler is running next to the accelerating train.

He swings his pistol in a back-hand hammer blow, smashing the window with the butt.

Iris screams as Steckler lunges through the opening next to her like some uniformed nightmare and grabs her.

He is still running alongside pulling on her.

Trying to drag her right out through the window.

She struggles. Bites his beery hand.

He swears and legs go.

Then makes one last grab . . .

Gets his fingers into her long mane of hair.

Yanks on her. She comes half out the window, screaming.

Then . . . RIP!

The hair pulls off her head.

Steckler drops away, behind the speeding train, holding a red-haired wig in one hand.

He looks at it stupidly for a second, then raises his pistol and fires at Iris.

She jerks back through the window and drops to the floor.

A couple of shots hit the metal outside.

Iris has shot hair, platinum white. In it are a few of the many pins which held the wig securely in place.

She gasps for air in great shakey sobs. She hugs her knees and sits on the floor trembling, catching her breath.

STECKLER STANDS on the platform, watching the train disappear, as Engelman runs up.
Steckler looks at the wig in his hand, disgusted.
Then he notices a fine wire dangling from it.
He turns it in his hand and looks inside, at the cap.

CLOSE ON THE CAP inside the wig: there is an intricate network of sensors in a grid over the entire underside of the wig. The sensors are connected by wires, in a pattern like the veins of a leaf, bundling to a small, flat metal box, the size of a cigarette case.
It is a SQUID NET. The sensor array of a cortical recorder.
Iris was wired.

Steckler just stares at it, his eyes going crazy wide.
Engelman realizes what it is and blanches.
Oh shit, he says.

IT'S 4 AM. Lenny trudges up to the entrance to his apartment building. It is a two-story stucco place, built in the sixties.
Upgraded in recent years with heavy security gates and bars on the windows, neither of which help its already drab design.

He uses a worn key-card to release the solenoid lock at the front gate.
There is no response. He tries it again. Nothing.
Frustrated, he pulls on the steel bars. The gate opens.
He notices that the lock has been forced with a crowbar, leaving useless twisted metal. Great.

He walks across the center court of the ratty building.
The pool furniture is in the pool. Leaves floating on top.
Graffiti marks the walls. Gang tags. One of the doors looks like somebody opened it with an axe.

The pool lights give the place an eerie, dead glow.
Can our slick Lenny really live in this dump?

Through a barred window we see Lenny approaching.
The sound of Lenny's OUTGOING MESSAGE is heard and
we see his answering machine in the F.G.
The beep. We hear a woman's voice . . . Iris.
She is begging him to pick up.
Through the window we see Lenny fishing in his pocket for
his keys.

CUT TO Iris at a payphone in the cold light of an all-night
gas station.
She tells Lenny she's in trouble and she really needs to talk
to him.
There's no one else she can trust. It's really important. She
needs his help.

INSIDE LENNY'S place, Iris' voice finishes the message
just as Lenny unlocks the door and comes in. All he hears is
that she'll call him back later.
He picks up the phone. Hears the click of her hang up.

IRIS rests her hand on the phone, hanging in its cradle. She
seems dazed, deflated, out of options. She looks around nervously, scanning the street. No cops in sight. She fishes in
the purse on her belt for some more quarters. Feeds them
into the phone and dials.
She takes a deep breath, listening to it ring.

LENNY doesn't stop to play back Iris' message, or any of
the twenty others on his machine. He just deadbolts the door
and locks a steel bar across the doorframe.

Lenny sets down his Haliburton and crosses the room

toward the kitchen. He becomes more stealthy in his movements . . . like he's sneaking up on the kitchen.

He silently opens a drawer and reaches inside.

His hand comes out holding a gun.

He reaches for the light . . . and snaps it on suddenly.

In the light half a dozen cockroaches freeze in or near the sink, which is piled up with a weeks' worth of dirty dishes.

Lenny aims his weapon swiftly.

SPANG! A suction-cup tipped plastic dart splatters one of the beasts against the tile behind the sink.

Lenny cheers like his team just scored. He lives for this.

We see the truth of his reality.

Lenny's crib is a shit-box. It is a standard one-bedroom, barely furnished. A couple of chairs. Swap meet couch. No art, no personal touches on the walls.

There are cardboard boxes full of tech gear stacked in the corners.

Some unidentified electronics components are piled on a table, with cables strung across the floor and into the bedroom.

God knows what this stuff is.

There is aluminum foil taped to all the windows.

Fast food cartons, empty Coke cans, pizza boxes, etc. are everywhere.

The fridge, revealed when he gets some ice for the vodka he pours himself, contains almost nothing edible.

This is the bachelor apartment from hell.

High-tech low-life.

He goes into the bedroom. There is a mattress on the floor. Clothes strewn everywhere. More boxes. More electronic gear, on a shelf made from a board laid across two cinder blocks.

The room is dominated by racks of tapes . . . squid tapes.

The apartment is a place where Lenny sleeps, and that's all. His life is outside, on the street. His car and his clothes are all he has. He is living in a balloon . . . an illusion he creates for others.

Lenny takes off his clothes and hangs them over a chair.
He sits on the bed in his underwear, looking now lonely and depressed. This is the private Lenny, who has dropped his street face. He lives from day to day, in the energy of the moment, and when the day is over . . . he has nothing. No plans. No dreams. Nothing to look forward to but another day of the hustle.

He sits cross-legged on the bed with his back against the wall.
Then he takes a cortical playback deck from the floor next to him and sets it on the bed. He raises the trode-set and places it carefully on his head.

He fishes around in a shoebox among a bunch of tapes, squinting at the hand-written dates and descriptions. We can't read much of his scrawl, but what all the tapes in the box seem to have in common is the word FAITH, printed on them clearly.

He selects one and inserts it in the deck. Makes some minute adjustments. Like an audiophile tweaking the EQ.
Then he rests his finger on the PLAY button.
Sips his vodka. Leans back. Closes his eyes.
And hits PLAY.

PLAYBACK SEQUENCE/POV:

We are moving along the Venice boardwalk, following a YOUNG WOMAN on rollerblades. By our motion, it is obvious that we are on rollerblades too, and not doing so

well. The woman is laughing, turning circles around us,
cracking up at our discomfort.
We hear Lenny's voice complaining a mile a minute, and
we realize the POV is is. The girl takes our hands, skating backward, towing us along the boardwalk. It is a
sunny afternoon, and it is the usual boardwalk freak-
show all around us.

The woman is FAITH JUSTIN, but lately she just goes by
FAITH (like Cher, Madonna, etc.). She is a singer, and
Lenny is desperately in love with her. It's not hard to see
why. She is beautiful, in an alive, dynamic way. Her hair
is a wild dark mane, and her eyes are spectacular . . .
intense. She moves with a lithe, sinuous grace. She is
dressed in shorts and a halter top, showing lots of her
ivory skin.
We are staring at her eyes instead of concentrating on
skating.
Whammo! The POV spins and we are sitting, looking up
at Faith as she circles, laughing. She skates over to help
us up.

CUT TO LENNY, on his bed, smiling. We don't know if
this tape is from a year ago or yesterday, or where Faith
is now. She might be dead, or she might walk in the door.
He punches a button on the deck.

BACK TO POV. The image goes into a kinetic blur of
digital hash . . . FAST FORWARD.
It goes back to normal running speed and we are sitting
on the steps of a decrepit stucco apartment building two
blocks from the beach, taking off our rollerblades. We
get up and follow Faith up the stairs to a second floor
apartment. We go inside. It is small and funky. You get
the impression they are living together.

Music is playing, a disc player she left on. Bob Marley
singing "Three Little Birds." Faith, covered with a sheen
of sweat, sways to the music as she goes into the bedroom. We follow her.

She comes out of the small bathroom with a towel, starts
to dry off.
We move up behind her and take the towel away.
Lenny's voice says he likes her better sweaty.
We see Lenny standing behind Faith in the mirror over
the dresser. Behind them is the messy, unmade bed. Sunlight comes in the window lighting up Faith like she is
in a spotlight.
Lenny puts his arms around her and they sway together
to the music. He runs his fingers in lazy circles over her
sweaty belly. He leans down and licks the sweat off her
shoulder, all the while watching her in the mirror. We
see past her shoulder to the reflected image of both of
them in the mirror. Their eyes meet in the mirror.

They both watch as Lenny slides his hand up under her
halter and caresses her nipples. She moans softly, re-
sponding. She turns to him, and our POV shifts directly
to her. She is right in front of us, in TIGHT CLOSE UP.
The intimacy is powerful. She closes her eyes and gets
even closer, kissing Lenny.

She opens her eyes, and laughingly busts him for keeping
his eyes open during the kiss. She knows how visual he
is . . . how that is a big part of his turn on. He looks from
her, inches away, back to the mirror, seeing them both
together full length . . . a voyeur recording his voyeurism
through his own eyes, so he can replay and relive the moment.

Lenny's hands pull her halter over her head. Faith pulls

up on Lenny's T-shirt, and we see it go over our eyes, blocking the view for a moment. Faith kisses Lenny's bare chest. We are looking down at her, looking down across our body, Lenny's body, as Faith kisses lower, kneeling in front of us.
She looks up, meeting our gaze. Her eyes sparkle with mischievous lust.
Faith unbuckles our belt and slowly unbuttons the fly of our jeans. Her hands pull down on the pants and we—

CUT TO LENNY in the here and now. Lost in playback memory bliss. He inhales sharply behind a wave of electronically recorded pleasure.

BACK TO POV. Lenny pulls Faith up to his face, kissing her. We lead her to the bed. We lie down together in a pool of sunlight which slashes across the tangled sheets. We see his hands helping her pull off her shorts. We kiss our way down her body, her creamy skin filling our field of view. We look up and see her looking down at us with smiling eyes.
We move below her navel and—

CUT TO LENNY, lost in the swirl of sensation. He touches his tongue to his fingertip.

IN POV we move back up her body. Supporting ourselves on straight arms, we look down at her as we enter her. She gasps and closes her eyes, grabbing the headboard with both hands. She rocks with the rhythm of our thrusts. It builds in intensity and she cries out, the tendons in her neck standing out. There is only the sound of gasping breaths, the creaking bed frame.

CUT TO LENNY, reliving the past, under the electrodes.

He reacts to the past orgasm. The tape ends.

Lenny slowly takes off the trodes.
There is a tiny tear at the corner of his eye. He seems deso-
late and very alone in his bleak room.

2:14 PM, December 30

Lenny cracks an eye. Looks at the cheap alarm clock sitting on a cardboard box next to his bed.
Sunlight comes like lasers through a couple of gaps around the edges of the aluminum foil over the window.

TIGHT ON LENNY'S TV coming on. His companion during the "morning" routine.
He goes to the fridge in his underwear. Opens it.
Nothing for breakfast.

On the TV, 90 percent ignored by him, is a news program.
Something about a religious cult whose members, which number in the thousands, have given away all their belongings and gathered in the desert near Needles, California, for some kind of Rapture. They all expect to get beamed up on the Eve of Judgment . . . tomorrow night.
The two news anchors at the station do their best to remain professional as they comment on the video clip of people sitting out in the middle of nowhere singing and praying.

Lenny finds a raspberry popsicle in the back of the freezer.
He has this for breakfast as he goes to the closet and starts picking out his clothes for the day.

This is a ceremony he observes carefully.
In his closet is a small selection of pretty good clothes.
He lays out a shirt and jacket combo.
Starts laying ties up against them. Humming to himself.

Lenny scowls at the tie he has chosen. Puts it back on the hanger. Gets another. Nods to himself.

CUT TO a transformed Lenny, driving through the Thursday evening traffic. It is about five o'clock: dusk.
Lenny looks slick . . . his look dialed-in.
This is Lenny on the move. Seizing the day. Talking on the phone, setting up an appointment. We sense that the hustle is what keeps him going . . . something he needs, that he does well . . . an immediacy he can immerse himself in. There's money to be made. Dreams to sell. Souls to X-ray.

On the radio, we hear a late-breaking story: the bodies of two men found early this morning under the Hollywood freeway have been identified as rap-music artist Jeriko One and another member of his band. The second man was known in the music world as "Replay," born James Polton. Both men were shot repeatedly, in what police are characterizing as an "execution-style" killing. The body of an as yet unidentified woman was found with them, also shot numerous times. Police earlier said that the killings appear to be gang-related. Jeriko One, whose latest album has sold over a million copies, recently used his music popularity to become a vocal activist on inner-city issues . . .

As this news story plays like a kind of voice over, we drive past scenes of LA deterioration. Homeless people wandering. Gang members riding around in cars. Helicopters circling.

Lenny has to stop at a police check-point set up on Santa Monica Boulevard. He doesn't pause in his cellular conversation. The bored cop flicks his eye over Lenny and waves him through.

The city is settling into night.
Neon and streetlights coming on.
Lenny pulls into the parking lot of a bar called THE

CORAL LOUNGE. He gets out of the BMW with his Haliburton and sets the car's alarm.

INSIDE THE CORAL LOUNGE Lenny cruises among the early regulars. Once again he seems to know everybody.

The decor is sort of Polynesian. Goofy tropical motif murals on the walls. The bartender, BOBBY, wears a Hawaiian shirt.
We see that the place has a mixed bag of customers, including upwardly mobile low-life who have graduated from the streets and use it as a kind of office. It is a crossroads for druggies, upscale hookers, junior entertainment suits slumming after a day in the pressure cooker.

Lenny sits at the bar and orders a drink.
A guy he knows named FABRIZIO, who works as a salesman at a Ferrari dealership, comes over and puts his hand on Lenny's shoulder. Fabrizio says he has a guy that wants to talk to him, and nods his head at a booth nearby. The guy in question is dressed LA power-casual: jeans, topsiders, knit-shirt under Italian jacket. Looks like money to Lenny.

Fabrizio reminds him as they cross the room that he gets 10 percent of any action for the introduction.

Lenny presses flesh with the guy, whose name turns out to be GRAEME KEITH. He's an entertainment attorney that Fabrizio sold some cars to over the years. Now he's interested in what Lenny has to sell.

Lenny asks the guy if he's a cop. Keith says no. Lenny laughs it off, says he knows, but he's gotta ask. *My second question I gotta ask, so we get our bearings here . . . have you ever jacked in? Have you ever wiretripped?*

No, Keith says.

A virgin mind, Lenny says with a winning grin.
We see Lenny go to work on the guy. Very charming. Tells him how the rig works, how the whole thing got started, with Federal intelligence agencies.

The guy wants to show he's cool, that he knows a bit about it. So he fills in part of the story. How SQUID technology was used by law enforcement to replace the audio-only body wire. How the current booming black market got started, etc.

Lenny says, *I see you've done your homework, so you know already that the effects are harmless, done in moderation like anything, and that this bullshit over a public health risk is just bullshit. So I'm guessing you're past the home-work stage, what you want now is to try it out. Am I right? Guy like you, a mover and a shaker, a plugged-in guy, wants to taste all of life there is. You drive Ferraris? You know that feeling when you shift from second to third in a 308? How do you explain that to somebody? You can't. You gotta experience it. That's what life is all about. Being there. Well that's what this is. You're there. You're doing it, seeing it, hearing it . . . feeling it.*

What kinda things, exactly? Keith asks, hooked like a carp.

Whatever you want. Who do you want to be, today? I'm as-suming a guy like you, you wanna go skiing you go skiing. That's not what you're interested in here. It's about the stuff you can't have. Right? The forbidden fruit.

Fabrizio chimes in with, *Lenny gives people their heart's de-sire. Ain't that right, Lenny? He's like some kinda Santa*

Claus of the Subconscious. All you gotta do is sit on his lap and tell him what you need.

Lenny goes on . . . *You wanna take a walk to the dark end of the street? The stuff you could never do . . . but sometimes you think about. You say . . . I wonder what that other guy's life is like. If I could just walk in his skin for twenty minutes. That guy running into a liquor store with a .357 magnum in his hand, feeling the adrenaline pumping through his veins, every nerve tight like a guitar string, feeling shit scared but so alive it's like red hot and ice cold at the same time. Or that other guy, the one with the drop-dead Philippino girlfriend, wouldn't you like to be that guy for twenty minutes . . . the right twenty minutes. You're married, I see the ring . . . so now there's so much of life you give up, sometimes you feel like a prisoner . . . but you don't have to. You can have it all. Anything you want. You want a girl, you want two girls, I don't know what your thing is or what you're curious about . . . you want a guy? You want to be a girl? See what that feels like? You want a nun to tie you up? It's all doable. You just gotta remember the brain is the most important sexual organ.*

Talk to me about costs, here.

Okay. Well it's a hardware-software kinda proposition. First you need a playback deck, which I'm going to get for you at my cost, since my thing is the software.

Clips.

That's right. Very good. I get the clips. I have a very select clientele, but I'm willing to take you on since you're a friend of Fabrizio's here and we go back.

How much for the deck?

*A businessman. I like that. Listen, before we get into num-
bers, I want you to know what we're talking about here. This
isn't like TV only better. This is life. It's a piece of somebody's life. This isn't like anything you've ever done before,
and I want you to try it . . . you're gonna go apeshit. I got a
deck in my case here, you can try a couple of sample experiences—*

What? Right here?

*Naw, come with me, we'll get some privacy going, you can
check this out. Fabrizio, why don't you get another round,
we'll be back in five.*

Lenny gets up and Keith follows him.
They go down a short corridor to the men's room and Lenny
checks to see if it's empty, then locks the door and puts his
Haliburton up on the sink. Pops it open.

OUTSIDE THE CORAL LOUNGE. It is full night now. We
see a figure move stealthily from the shadows and approach
Lenny's car. A woman with jet-black hair, wearing jeans and
a coat. It is Iris, obviously trying to look as different as possible from last night.
She has a black eye, which she has tried to cover with make-
up.

Looking furtively around, she crosses to Lenny's car and
tries the door handles. It's locked. She looks at the bar. De-
bates going in to find him.

Iris takes a piece of paper from her pocket and writes him
a note: LENNY, HELP ME. PLEASE. I'LL CALL YOU
TONIGHT. IRIS.
Then she takes something else from her pocket, a squid
tape. She wraps the note around it, holding it in place with a

hair-tie, and drops it through the two-inch gap in the sunroof of Lenny's BMW.

It lands on the seat, and bounces off onto the floor.

Shit, she says, squinting through the windshield, trying to see where it landed.

She glances around, looking totally paranoid.

Iris sees a police car coming down the street.

She turns her back and waits, petrified, as it passes. When it is gone she sags against Lenny's car. Her knees buckle and she slides down, with her back against the car door, crying quietly in the shadows.

Afraid to move.

IN THE MEN'S ROOM Lenny adjusts the position of the playback headset on Keith's head. He selects a tape and puts it in the deck.

Grins at the lawyer, who nods nervously. Lenny's got the guy sitting on the counter next to the sink. He tells him to close his eyes and relax. Then he punches PLAY.

We don't see what the guy is experiencing. Just his reactions. First he jerks . . . then his mouth drops open. He gasps and starts to breathe rapidly. He puts his hands on his body and "feels" it wonderingly.

Then one hand raises reflexively, in response to something on the tape. He groans and tilts his head down, as if looking down, but his eyes are closed. He gasps . . . and Lenny punches PAUSE.

The lawyer opens his eyes. Lenny grins knowingly.

You were just an eighteen-year-old girl taking a shower. Are you beginning to see the possibilities here?

The guy is clearly shocked and intoxicated by the experience.

IN THE BAR a man in his late thirties enters. He has longish hair and hasn't shaved in days. He wears a long army jacket, which adds additional bulk to his massive frame. He walks to the bar with a slight limp. The bartender sees him coming and moves casually down to him.
Where is he? the man says.
The bartender looks toward the men's room and the man nods.

ON LENNY and the lawyer, coming out of the can.
They move down the short hallway. Lenny, his voice lowered, is saying *let's sit down and talk about getting you set up.*

The door to the women's restroom is whipped open and the guy in the army jacket comes out behind Lenny.
He grabs him and hurls him face-first against the wall, sticking a .45 against the back of his head and saying *don't move, you miserable puke! That's right!* . . . and kicking his feet apart, keeping him off balance.

The lawyer splits in a hurry, pretending he's not with Lenny. Fabrizio gets a whiff of what's going on and goes after him. Rats deserting the ship.
Lenny whips around, swearing. He roughly shoves the other man back against the wall by the payphones.
The guy in the army jacket doesn't resist because now he's laughing too hard. He puts the .45 back in his waistband.

Gotcha, the guy says.

Goddammit, Max! I was with a client, you dumb motherfucker. Shit, look . . . now the guy's outta here. Son of a bitch.

Come on, Lenny, MAX says, let me buy you a drink.

They go to the bar. Max roars greetings to several regulars, stopping conversations all around the room, instantly becoming the center of attention. They call him "Mad Max." He says *fuckin A right, I might just kill every man in here. But first I'm buyin' my buddy here a drink.*

Max lurches onto a barstool and hunches there like a misanthropic bear, pounding the bartop until he gets what he wants, which is quick service from Bobby, the bartender, and *none of your well-shit tequilla . . . gotta be Tres Generaciones! Double shots!*

Mad Max is MAX PELTIER (which he himself mispronounces as "Pelcher"), Lenny's best friend. Max is also an ex-cop.
A homicide detective who's out on a disability pension. Some shitbird shot him in the head with a .22 and pushed him over a freeway guardrail. He fell 30 feet and shattered two vertebra.
Woke up three days later in a hospital bed, with a .22 shot floating around in his brainpan somewhere, and a bad headache. Imagine how pissed off he was.

Now he supposedly works as a private detective, but doesn't seem to do much but drink for a living. Though it never seems to affect him.

On the plus side he's intelligent, articulate, funny and acidly cynical. He has a kind of cheeriness, as if the completely fucked-up state of the world is a source of endless amusement for him. Max believes in the lowest and most venal interpretation on any given event and is seldom disappointed. He is also a sort of street philosopher, given to long rambling tracts on the state of things.

He can make friends with anyone in a heartbeat, and has a

very low tolerance for bullshit. He's loud, boorish, thinks he's always right, and is the kind of capable guy you'd call first in a jam.

He and Lenny go way back. Worked together in Vice, before Max made Homicide and Lenny went onto the surveillance team.

Lenny's still pissed off about losing a sale. He's tight on cash and it's going to be a big weekend.

Max tells him to *relax, there's a lot more fish in the sea. And nobody knows how to work 'em like you do, pal. You could sell a goddamn rat's asshole for a wedding ring! Hey, that's a nice tie, Lenny.*

Thanks, Max.

D'you always have to dress like a fucking pimp?

Look, this tie cost more than your whole wardrobe. It's the one thing that stands between me and the jungle.

Maybe, now I think about it, you are a pimp . . . some kinda eelectronic techno-pimp.

He calls Lenny an input junkie. Says the biggest problem is he's sampling his own merchandise too much.
Says, *You should knock that shit off, or you're going to fry your brain, amigo. Hey Bobby! Another shooter right here.* (to Lenny) *I like the simple, old-fashioned kind of slow death. Call me a traditionalist. Hey, you seen Faith lately?*

Lenny gets uncharacteristically glum.

Naw, she's still with that music slick. Philo Gant.

*Look, Lenny, she's been with that shitbird for six months,
this is not news. It might be time for you to consider moving
on. I hate to see you pining away like this . . . it makes me
want to vomit, frankly. I mean sure, Faith was by far the
most outstanding woman a guy like you could ever hope to
get, but it's over.*

Thanks, Max.

At the door, Iris slips inside and starts making her way
toward them.
She comes up to Lenny looking pale. He and Max both greet
her. Max asks her what happened to her eye.

Nothing, she says. *Lenny can I talk to you?*

Sure, he says, meaning here and now.
No, I mean, just you.
Fuck me. Max says and gets up, crossing the room to some
people he knows at a booth.

What's going on? he asks. *You need money? You want some
wire work?*

Iris is nervous, evasive.
She tells Lenny she thinks she is being followed, watched
. . . won't tell him why. But something's going on. She needs
his help. He's the only one she can trust.

He thinks her pimp beat her up. He's seen this shit a million
times. Doesn't have time for some strung-out hooker's problems.

She says she put something in his car, that he needs to see
right away. It's important. She didn't want to come in, be-

cause a lot of people know her here, but then she decided she better talk to him now.

He asks her what's going on. Not really paying attention, scanning the room for business. He waves to someone coming in, that he needs to talk to.

She doesn't want to talk in the bar. She needs to get out. She's starting to freak.
He finally realizes that he should be listening to her, that however trivial her problems may be to him, she is a human being and he should help her if it doesn't cost him too much time or money.
She warns him to keep an eye on Faith, she may be in danger, but can't tell him more.

Now she's got his attention. Iris used to be a friend of Faith's, though they have moved far apart in recent years.

Lenny throws some money on the bar and takes her by the arm. They head for the door. They can talk in his car.

As they go out the door Iris sees a Black-and-White pull up across the street. Lenny walks on, talking. He turns in mid-sentence . . .
Iris is gone.

He looks around. Can't figure where she went. He shrugs. Just another strung-out street loser. He forgets about Iris a second later when he sees that a tow truck has got his BMW on the hook. What the fuck?

He runs to the guy . . . thinking it's some bullshit parking thing.
Finds out the guy is a repo man.

The guy says Lenny's missed five payments and the car is going back.

Lenny never figured they'd find him. His apartment is under another name. Telephone is unlisted. He takes his mail at a P.O. box.

The repo man looks like a biker only meaner. He jerks the hydraulic lever and the BMW's front end comes off the ground. Lenny grabs the guy's beefy arm and the guy whips around, putting a .38 in Lenny's face.

Lenny shouts *Oh, yeah! That's the answer, two million years of human evolution and that's the best idea you can come up with?*

He calms down and starts working the guy.

Look, let's be human beings here. You look like a guy that doesn't mind playing it smart if he can do it clean? Am I right? Look, whatya get to pull in a car? Two hundred? Two fifty? I'll pay you more not to. I'm gonna give you three fifty, right now. All you gotta do is take it off the hook and say you came by and your mark wasn't here. Simple. Make a few bucks extra. Do a good deed. Am I right?

The guy's thinking. You can tell by the way his little piggy eyes turn into slits.

You got the cash on you?

I was going to write you a check, if that's—

The guy is getting into his truck.

Okay, I totally respect that call. Cash makes sense. I got it right in there, right inside the bar, a buddy of mine owes

*me . . . I can see you're pressed for time, just give me two
minutes . . . here keep my watch for collateral. I go inside
and cop the money, come right out.*

He hands the guy his watch.

It's a Rolex. Be right back. Two minutes.

Lenny gets to the door of the Coral Lounge and looks back.
The driver is in his truck, pulling out of the lot.
Lenny runs after the truck, chasing his own car up the street
on foot, but he can't catch it.
Prick!!

Lenny walks back to the bar. He sets his case up on the
trunk of a car in the lot and pops it open. He takes out a tiny
digital cellular phone and dials a number. While it's ringing
he takes another, identical pseudo-Rolex out of the Haliburton and slips it on.

CUT TO a hand pulling a little digital cellular out of a black
jacket. Follow the hand and phone to the face of a black
woman. LORNETTE "MACE" MASON. Late twenties.
Striking features. Hair pulled back tight to her skull. She is
driving, but we don't see the car, or anything but her face
and some moving lights outside.

Hello?

Mace, what's goin' on?

Hey, Lenny. Whatup?

*Listen, Mace, I was wondering if you could swing by the
Coral. I gotta talk to you.*

Mace smirks knowingly.

Yeah? So what happened to your car this time?

BACK INSIDE Lenny is telling Max what happened.

LENNY
... so I'm trying to get this prick repo guy to drop it off the hook and he sticks a .38 in my face.

MAX
So? D'ja pull your piece?

LENNY
I ain't carrying.

MAX
Man, I cannot feature that about you. An ex-cop that doesn't carry. In LA? It's embarrassing, compadre. I oughta not be seen with you.

LENNY
(shrugs) I'm still on probation. Can't afford to get popped with one on me.

MAX
Yeah, but don't you feel exposed? Like your pants are down around your ankles? I'd come unglued, myself, walking around this city.

LENNY
I just don't like guns, Max. You know that.

MAX
Yeah, I remember. So let's go get the cocksucker.

LENNY
Naw, forget it. He'll be at the impound yard by

now. And I don't have the dinero to bail the thing
out anyway.

Max notices what's on the TV behind the bar and yells at
Bobby to turn it up.

It is a newscast about the killing of Jeriko One. We see file-
footage of Jeriko and his band, the Prophets of Light, from
interviews and some of their videos. The story is about reaction among Jeriko's fans, who are mostly black inner-city
kids. Jeriko One used his music as a political tool, becoming
an outspoken leader . . . an opponent of the LAPD and the
city government.

File shot: Jeriko One at an outdoor rally. Yelling that *their
social programs are not working! Their plan is not working! The mayor and the city council sit up in their offices,
and their shit ain't working . . . these people are rearrang-
ing deck chairs on the Titanic. And the millenium is coming . . . yeah, it's coming. The big 2K coming and when it
does, there's gonna be a new day, and not the one they
thinkin' of!*

We see that Jeriko One had a messianic quality, an aura of
almost religious power. In the file footage the crowd is going
wild.
The shot is followed by one of the murder scene . . . cops
milling around, yellow plastic over the crumpled forms on
the ground.

Max hoists a glass to the end of the world.

Don't start, Lenny says.

See, that guy got it, Max says. *Before they capped his sorry
ass. He saw the writing on the wall. Nostradamus got it,*

three hundred years ago. He gave us until the end of this century. It's all coming down. Look around man. The system is collapsing . . . the criminal justice system, the health system, we're bailing out the banking system, the whole fucking economy is collapsing, not just here but all around the world.

Max downs the shooter.

Every paradigm on Earth is falling apart at the same time . . . every system, vision, constitution, revelation . . . is breaking down. Being toppled or abandoned . . . all at the same time! And you know what really scares me? There's no new ideas. Everything's been done. Rock music, punk music, rap music, techno, techno-Mex . . . long hair, short hair . . . no hair. Doesn't it feel like everything's been tried? Whaddya do that's new? Something new in art? Forget it. Somebody somewhere has done it. Clothes, music . . . it's all been done. How you gonna make it another thousand years, for Chrissake? I'm telling you, it ain't happening. We used it up. It's over. You hungry?

They order some nachos.

OUTSIDE A BLACK LIMO pulls into the lot. It is a Continental armored stretch, downsized from today's standards. The door opens and Mace gets out. She is compactly built, dressed in black slacks and a conservative black jacket. Heavy rubber-soled shoes, like cop shoes. She glances around as she heads for the Coral Lounge entrance, the unconscious sweeping gaze of a security professional.

INSIDE, MACE looks around and spots Lenny and Max at the bar, and goes over, greeting them both casually. She takes a big glob of Lenny's nachos and shovels them in her mouth as she sits next to him.

Lenny asks if she can give him a ride to a couple of places because his wheels got jerked due to some kind of computer error at the bank which he won't be able to straighten out until the morning.

She says no way.

Mace tells him that she's already pulled a 12-hour shift and she has one more quick pick-up and drop, and then she's done for the day.

Says she's gotta grab some sleep.

It's gonna be a big night tomorrow night with all the New Year's parties.

Lenny begs her, using all his charm and persuasion.

We sense that they are friends and that it is not the first time Lenny has tried to suck her in to his nocturnal rounds.

What part of <u>*NO*</u> *don't you understand?* she says.

He offers her a percentage of the money he makes tonight.

Mace says she doesn't want his filthy money and we realize she does not approve of what Lenny does for a living.

Finally she relents and offers him a ride to her next pick-up, which is at the St. James in Hollywood, and he can get a taxi from there.

He says sure and they leave together.

CUT TO MACE AND LENNY in her limo, on the road. Lenny sits up front with her while they cruise the night streets.

We get a little background on Mace, and get the sense that she has been friends with Lenny for some time. He asks about her son, ZANDER, who's five already. Lenny likes Zander.

They drive through the streets. They see an unrolling pageant of crime, cops, and urban decay. More sense of how far LA has fallen. They go through a police checkpoint, which resembles the border patrol highway-stops south of San Diego.

Cops look in the cars with flashlights as they creep through.

Mace glances at his Haliburton and starts giving him a hard time about his work. She met him when he was a cop, and he seemed like a special guy, with some real insight into people, and now he's just running around selling this sit. Breaking the law.

When Zander asks what he does she has to lie.

> **LENNY**
>
> Look, you just tell him I'm performing a humanitarian service. I probably save lives.

> **MACE**
>
> I wanna hear this part.

> **LENNY**
>
> Okay, some executive in Century City is bored with his life, bored with his wife, itching to cut loose . . . what does he do?

> **MACE**
>
> Picks up a hooker.

> **LENNY**
>
> Yeah, or he has a smokin' one-nighter with some girl he meets in the bar at a sales convention. Then he goes around for months, paranoid that he's got AIDS, that he'll infect his wife. He's torn up. Needs years of therapy. And what if he really does catch something and totally destroys his life?

MACE
Price he pays for being a scumsucking pig.

LENNY
Everybody needs to take a walk to the dark end of
the street once in while, it's what we are. But it's
just now the risks are outta line. The streets are a
war zone. And sex can kill you. So I sell this guy
what he needs. Almost as good as the real thing,
and a lot safer. And it keeps him from jumping his
tracks.

MACE
It's porno, Lenny. Face it, you're a sleaze mer-
chant.

LENNY
No, wrong . . . I sell *experiences.* All kinds of experiences. Sexual experiences are just part of it. You
put on the trodes in the safety of your own home
and you get to know what it feels like to ride with
a gang, or get in a bar fight, or walk around in
drag, or do the nasty with a thousand-dollar-a-
night call girl or some shanky teen-hooker or a
West Hollywood boy hustler. Whatever you want.
You're safe from injury, safe from arrest, and safe
from disease.

MACE
Buncha techno-perve jerkoffs.

LENNY
Man, you are so unenlightened. My customers are
people with a lot to lose . . . you know, they got
high-paying jobs, high-visibility, professional
status . . . some a them are celebrities . . .

> MACE

Yeah, what celebrities?

> LENNY

That guy from the news.

> MACE

He doesn't count as a celebrity. He does the weather.

> LENNY

That counts.

> MACE

Lenny, this shit's illegal.

> LENNY

Well, it's a gray area.

> MACE

It's not a gray area. It's a misdemeanor area. That's why I've had to come down and bail your sorry pale ass out of jail at two o'clock in the morning twice in the last two months.

> LENNY

Look, it's not like I'm dealing crack here.

> MACE

What's the difference?

> LENNY

Okay, do me a favor, Mace. Just pull over at the next junior high you see, would you, I have some bondage and S and M tapes I have to sell.

She pulls into the St. James Hotel and tells the doorman she

has a pickup. A Mr. Fumitsu. Lenny gets out with his case and is standing next to Mace as her client, a Japanese executive, comes out to the car.
Fumitsu tells her he is going to a nightclub on the west side.

As Mace is opening the limo's back door, Lenny brashly shakes Fumitsu's hand and tells him he is from BLS (the company Mace works for), and that he will be riding along as part of their regular driver-evaluation program, if Mr. Fumitsu doesn't mind.

It's routine, we do it every six months to make sure our drivers are courteous and professional at all times, so that VIP clients such as yourself are always treated as honored guests. Of course all our drivers are bonded security specialists, trained in defensive combat, and this car is fully armored, with bullet-resistant glass all around.

Lenny pats the Lincoln with possessive pride.
Mace scowls at Lenny and gives him a look like "don't do this" but Lenny just blusters on, telling Fumitsu to just relax, and pretend he's not even here. He'll just sit up front and take notes.

Mace gets in and Lenny opens his case, pulling out a small notebook. He grins at her and she cracks up in spite of herself.

Lenny turns to Fumitsu almost right away and begins telling him about what an excellent choice he has made for his evening's entertainment. He asks if Fumitsu has ever been to the club before.
Fumitsu, in broken English, says it was recommended to him.
Lenny soon has worked the conversation around to another club, called CLUB MONDO 2000, which might be even more

what the executive is looking for. He actually talks him into changing his plans and going to Mondo 2000. Mace rolls her eyes. She can't believe this shit.

She's hissing at Lenny under her breath that he is going to get her fired.

CUT TO a few minutes later. Lenny is in the back with Fumitsu. They are laughing uproariously. Lenny says something in Japanese and they laugh again. Fumitsu likes him. Lenny opens his briefcase. Winks at Mace in the mirror.

Now she's pissed off.

CUT TO the limo pulling up at Club Mondo 2000.

Inside, Fumitsu is pulling off Lenny's playback trodes and smiling. Apparently the Japanese are very hip to the playback underworld, and Lenny makes a sale right there.

Mace can't believe this shit.

She opens the door for Fumitsu and asks him if he wants her to wait. He says he will call for pickup.

Lenny gives Mace a shiteating grin.

She waits until Fumitsu is out of sight and then grabs him by the tie.

He is surprised that she is really angry.

She says every time she sees him, she feels slimed afterward.

Their friendship is based on her doing favors for him. And this stunt could get her fired. Making an illegal sale right in her car.

He tells her to relax. *The guy's having a great time. He'll probably recommend her company to all his pals.*

Mace is also pissed off because she knows why Lenny just had to come to Mondo 2000 . . .

Yeah, because I have business here, he says.

Uh huh, right. It doesn't have anything to do with Faith being here.

Oh, is she here? he says innocently.

They hear shouting and look over at a scene a few yards away. Next to their armored limos two rich guys are yelling at each other, drunk. They are each backed up by two or three bodyguards . . . "private security specialists." Rich-guy posses. One R.G. swings on the other. The other's body-guards jump into it, grabbing the attacker. Now the first guy's security guys have to jump in to protect him. Pretty soon the bodyguards are duking it out and the two rich guys are standing back watching.

Lenny tells Mace he'll buy her a drink, now she's off the clock. She scowls but accompanies him inside. She doesn't know why she puts up with his shit.

Lenny and Mace enter the Club Mondo 2000.
They are greeted inside by two suited guys with metal de-tectors. Lenny and Mace barely notice as they are scanned, it's so routine most places these days. Mace shows her gun, a Sig-Saur 9mm, and her state carry permit. The security guys check her pistol like a coat, giving her a claim check.

They walk in.
MONDO is upscale and chic. Film types, music types, and rich-fucks in general. There is a bar, and a lounge with live music.

Through the crowd in the lounge Lenny spots a particular table. It seems to be in a pool of light all its own. Or maybe this is just in Lenny's mind. SLOW MOTION. Lenny watches a man at the table holding court, with a beautiful young woman sitting next to him.

The man is PHILO GANT, record producer and manager. He is mid-thirties, with dark intense eyes, and long hair in a ponytail. He is severely handsome, and hiply dressed in a studied eclectic-casual style.

The woman is FAITH JUSTIN. We recognize her from the playback as Lenny's ex-girlfriend. But now we are seeing a new "designed" Faith. Her hair has been dyed jet black, and frames her face in a wild tangle. She is wearing an expensive custom leather jacket over a sheer silk top slashed almost to her navel. She has on too much make-up, which gives her features a strange feral-doll quality. Faith looks like what she is, a rock-star wannabe. But the look is red-hot.

Gant and Faith are flanked on either side by an entourage consisting of music types, various hangers on, and Gant's personal security force of four.

Somebody says something to Faith and she turns slightly to look at Lenny. Their eyes meet for a moment. Then she coolly turns back to the conversation without a flicker of acknowledgment.

Mace scowls at the tableau and pulls Lenny toward the bar, reminding him that he is supposed to be buying her a drink. The following plays as they cross to the bar and sit down.

Forget her, Lenny.

She still loves me.

She thinks you're a bucket of dog vomit, Lenny. Trust me on this.

This is just something she's got to work through. She's a little confused about her life right now.

Whatever.

You don't understand what we have.

Had. Not have. See, have is present tense.

She's my destiny.

Your destiny? What're you . . . living in a Hallmark card? She's a hard-climber that dropped you like a used tampon when she got a better ride.

You'll see.

The bartender slides down to them, greeting Lenny by name.
FRASER LOVEJOY looks like a model, which he occasionally is when he's not tending bar at the 2000. Lenny tells him he may have a gig for him next week, that he'll give him a call.

Lenny turns to look across the room at Gant and Faith. He says, *Hey who's the new slab-o-meat in Gant's posse?*

Mace looks at the massively built bodyguard seated near Philo Gant and Faith.

That's Wade Beemer, he was a running back for the Rams in '96 and '97. He's been working security lately. I've seen him around. Didn't know he was with Gant.

The Rams . . . that's football right? Lenny says.

Fraser brings their drinks and says SKINNER was looking for him earlier. He points at a table nearby. Lenny grabs his drink and motions to Mace to follow him.

He crosses to the table and comes up behind Skinner, a plump guy with thinning hair who dresses too young, sitting with a pretty, stoned-looking girl and a young guy with slicked back hair and gold chains who looks like a freshman gigolo.

Skinner is a porno video producer.
Lenny greets him loudly as "The Skin Man" and slaps his palm.
He fingers Skinner's coat.

Red leather. Nice feminine touch.

Fuck you, Skinner laughs.

Lenny tells him he needs him to set up "a special."
A guy and two girls. The guy wears.

Trent yawns. *There's an original idea.*

Yeah, I know, Lenny says. *The girls have to be young, and no big tits . . . French tits, you know, like a champagne glass. And my client wants it fast.*

Trent pretends it's the last thing in the world he cares to do.
Tells Lenny he needs an advance, to lock the talent.
Lenny says forget it, he'll get somebody else.
Skinner grabs his arm.

I'll have it Monday. The usual price.

Page me when you got it, Lenny says.

Mace gets up. She tells Lenny whenever he's done with his squalid techno-perve business, she'll be waiting outside. He's got ten minutes and then she's gone.

Skinner laughs at Lenny's uptight friend. Lenny just shrugs it off.

The Skin Man says he just finished a video shoot with a couple of new girls, and he got them to do some squid stuff afterward, if Lenny's interested. Lenny shrugs . . . sure.

Skinner hands him a tape and Lenny opens his overcoat, revealing a playback deck clipped to his belt, next to his pager. He pops in the tape and glances around casually as he pulls out the trodes. He doesn't put the trode-set completely over his head . . . he just sort of hunches over the bar and touches a couple of the pads to his forehead.
"Sampling" the merchandise.
It looks like any drug buy in a public place.

CUT TO: POV of a woman writhing above us in ecstasy. Lovemaking in point-of-view.
We look down, see our body, a woman's body . . . our hands moving over the other woman's torso.
The image is dark, a primal impression.
The sound of harsh breathing, rustling sheets.

BACK TO LENNY, dropping the headset back in his pocket.
Yeah, I can use this, he says. But tell the girl to move her eyes slower next time. It's pretty jerky.
Skinner shrugs. Whattya expect, Marty fucking Scorsese? It was her first time, Lenny. Cut her some slack.

Skinner introduces the young guy, who has been watching

all this intently. Says this is EDUARDO, the guy I was telling you about.

Apparently Eduardo is going to wear in a "situation."

Lenny asks him if she's sure he wants to do it. The guy says *you're going to pay me 200 bucks to put on a hair-net and bang some beautiful girl. I don't know. I gotta think about this.*

Lenny gives him some pointers. LIke a coach before the game.

Okay, Eduardo, some tips here. Don't dart your eyes around, don't do any crank or anything that will give your eyeballs the jitters, it looks terrible. Don't look in the mirror, you ID yourself, then I gotta make an edit to take it out, and it ruins the moment. Plus the edits are jarring. Feels like getting slapped on the backside of your eyeballs. You got a half hour of tape. So gimme a little lead-in to the main event. It works better if there's a little tease. But don't bore the shit outta me. And most important of all . . . don't act natural. Don't fucking act *at all. Just completely forget the thing is on and do your thing, or it'll be dogshit. Trent, you gonna wire him up yourself?*

Yeah.

Okay, (to Eduardo) There's nothing to it. Trent'll set you up, put on the wig and all that. Wash your hair though, that fucking axle grease'll screw up the squid receptors.

What's all this squid *shit?*

Superconducting QUantum Interference Device. SQUID. Got it?

Yeah. Uh, sure.

Don't forget it. There's gonna be a test. Just kidding. Relax. Okay, the receptor rig . . . the part that goes on your head . . . sends an RF signal to the recorder. It's wireless. See, we call it "being wired," but there's no wire. So stick it in your jacket pocket and then hang the jacket over a chair next to the bed. Or wherever it is you're going to close escrow, know what I mean?

No problem.

A star is born, Lenny says.

CUT TO Lenny on the move, cruising through the crowd at the Club Mondo 2000. He just happens to pass Philo Gant's table. Pretends to see him for the first time.
Gant motions expansively.

Hey everybody, it's Lenny Nero.

Gant's right hand man, JOEY CORTO, smirks at Lenny. Corto is whipper thin, snappily dressed. His Rolex is real.
Lenny the Loser, Corto says.

Philo gives a cold little grin and says (pointedly) *Faith, do you know Lenny?*

Knock it off, Philo. Hello Lenny.

Hey, Faith.

Did you see Faith's video, Lenny?

The one with the water pouring down all over her in slow motion? Yeah. I thought it was overproduced. Faith's too good, she doesn't need all that shit. Any producer with the taste God gave an amoeba woulda figured that out.

We can see that Lenny and Philo don't care for each other. Gant and Lenny spar sarcastically. Faith tells them both to grow up.
She asks Lenny what he's doing here.

What am I doing here? Excuse me. I seem to recall it was me turned you on to this club in the first place.

Yeah, that's right, Lenny, Gant says, *And you introduced her to me here, as a matter of fact. I never thanked you, by the way. So . . . thanks. Now get the fuck out of here.*

Hey Gant, too bad about your guy, Jeriko. Tough break.

Fuck you, Nero. Show a little respect. The man was an important artist.

Yeah, and a good seller for your label. Which no doubt is why you're in mourning. But don't worry, his records'll go through the roof now he's dead. You'll make out. Faith, can I talk to you a second?

I don't think that's a good idea, Lenny, she says.

Gant glances at Joey Corto and says, *Joey, Nero was just leaving, I thought.*

Hey, I got something to say to her, alright?

Not alright. Good seeing you, Nero.

You're pretty insecure, Philo, you worried about her out of your sight for thirty seconds. You know, trust is an impor-

tant element of any relationship. (to Faith) I just gotta talk to you for one second.

We have nothing to talk about, Lenny.

Gant turns to Corto . . . Joey. Wade.

Corto gets up, motioning to the bodyguards. The biggest, WADE BEEMER, covers Lenny with his shadow. The second bodyguard is a woman, CONSTANCE. She is a massively built bodybuilder, who contrasts her hulking frame with a low-cut dress and pearls. Like a woman imitating a drag-queen, but definitely female . . . and somehow sexy and terrifying at the same time. The third bodyguard is DUNCAN, a not-too-bright classic arm-breaker.

Faith, call me, okay?

No, Lenny.

It's not about you and me. I just have to talk to you.

Corto motions to Wade and Duncan to grab Lenny. Wade gets him in a wrist-grip come-along hold and starts him moving toward the back of the club.

As they are marching Lenny through the crowd somebody coming the other way greets him.

Hey, Lenny!

Hey, Frank. Listen I can't stop right now, but I'll call you tomorrow about that thing we were talking about.

He's working the room even as he's getting dragged outside

to get the shit beat out of him. Wade and Duncan take Lenny out through the kitchen.

INSIDE, Faith turns to Philo and glares at him.

Leave him alone, Philo.

Relax, baby. They've just gonna make sure he gets to his car okay.

Corto moves off a few feet from the table and pulls out a small walkie-talkie. He gives Wade his instructions, which Wade gets in his secret-service type earpiece. Corto tells him to fuck Lenny up.
Ruin his New Year's.

OUTSIDE Wade leaves Duncan to watch the entrance to a dark alley behind the club. Wade walks Lenny back into the shadows of the alley. Lenny starts doing what he does best . . . talking.

Hey, I recognize you. You're Wade Beemer, right? You played for the Rams three or four years ago. Running back, am I right?

Beemer, who was about to go to work on Lenny, pauses.

Yeah, that's right.

I saw you play, man. You were good. Like a fucking freight train, I remember saying. So what happened? Injuries or what?

Bullshit politics.

It's always politics, isn't it?

Lenny starts to negotiate. Tries to get Beemer to cut him loose.

Wade says he has to do what Mr. Gant says.

We see Lenny wheeling and dealing . . . trying to work it out . . . says he'll pay him not to thrash him. Write him a check right now. Nobody needs to know. Wade won't take a check in exchange for a beating. Lenny gives Wade all his cash.

Wade is philosophical. Says, *We all have our roles to play . . . like nobody's doing anything to anybody . . . this is just happening.*

Lenny shrugs, says, *I know. But can we make a deal here?*

Wade says, *I have to do <u>something</u> or I'll get fired. It's not personal. Maybe I can go light. Stay away from the hands and the knees.*

Lenny agrees to the terms. He takes off his Armani jacket and hangs it nearby. He asks Wade to watch the eyes.

Wade takes his first swing.

CUT TO Mace waiting out front. She yawns and looks at her watch.

Lenny walks up to her, limping. He has a bloody nose.

She asks him what happened and he says, *I tripped on the stairs. They oughta get some lights back there. I should sue. Let's go.*

CUT TO a NIGHTVISION VIEW of Mace and Lenny getting into her car.

Burton Steckler, in plain clothes, lowers the surveillance device from his eyes. He is sitting in a car a block from the club, watching. As Mace and Lenny pull out he puts his car in gear and follows.

IN THE CAR, on the way to his next stop, a party in Hancock Park, Lenny asks Mace to stop so he can get in the backseat. Says it'll look better when he pulls up. She tells him if he wants to be back there, he's climbing through the divider window.

Lenny gets in the backseat and stretches out in luxury. Asks where the champagne is. She doesn't think it's all that funny. *Driving Mr. Lenny.*

BACK AT THE CLUB MONDO 2000 we see Faith and Gant. They don't exactly seem like a happy couple. Gant is clearly unsettled by Lenny. Wade comes back in and asks Gant about Lenny, who he is.
Gant says he's just a little weasel, a street hustler, nobody.
Since he's new to this entourage Wade is doing his homework, like any good security professional.

Then Gant gives a kind of 30-second profile on Lenny . . . ex–vice cop, a surveillance guy . . . one of those snoopers, always bugging people, wearing a wire, recording what you say, going through your trash . . . a maggot. He got into squid recording and got hooked on the stuff himself, then he got tossed off the force for dealing squid tapes after hours. Couldn't even make it as a cop. Lenny the loser. Panhandler of stolen dreams.

Coming from Gant it all sounds pretty sleazy. Of course he is painting the most negative picture because Faith is sitting there. He's rubbing her nose in it.

How does he know you, Mr. Gant? Wade asks.

Because Mr. Gant was one of Lenny's biggest clients, Faith says. *Mr. Gant likes to watch, don't you, baby? He used to buy everything Lenny had to sell. And the kinkier the better.*

That's right. Especially the ones of you.

Yeah, you liked those, didn't you. Probably even more than the real thing.

That's not true, baby. I'm much happier now that you're mine.

He grabs her behind the neck and kisses her fiercely. It seems less like passion than a public branding. She pulls back. Faith hates this, being treated like chattel. Gant treats her like a beautiful car, a Ferrari, something to draw approving looks from other men . . . and something over which he has total mastery and complete ownership.
We see at this moment that she does not love him, and that he probably knows that.
But the game has its own inertia.
And they both play the game.
They both get what they need out of it.

Faith wants to get out of the booth.
She tells Joey Corto to move.

Where you going? Philo says.

For a walk. You mind?

Constance, go with her.

Alone.

Gant grabs her arm and grips it tightly, pulling her down, close to him.

Look, what is this shit? I'm not about to have you wander-

ing around by yourself. Not with what's going on right now. Christ, use your head, Faith.

If you're so goddamn paranoid, maybe we should have just stayed home in our little beds.

Yeah, that wouldn't look too suspicious, would it?

Will you calm down? I'm going to the bathroom. Is that alright? You need to give me a hall pass?

He lets her go.

FAITH walks down a corridor, right past the ladies' room and into the kitchen. She goes out the back door of the club and walks around to the street. She gets into a taxi and tells the driver to head downtown.

She opens her purse and pulls out a handheld cellular. Recalls a preprogrammed number and pushes send.

LENNY hears the phone ringing in his briefcase and answers it.
He is surprised to hear Faith's voice.
She tells him to meet her backstage at the Retinal Fetish later. They can talk then. She has a gig there tonight. Her set starts at midnight.

Mace stops the car at a security checkpoint at the entrance to Hancock Park, which is now a closed, gated community.

I have a Mr. Nero for the party at 287 Briartree, Mace tells the guard. She has to really grit her teeth, playing Lenny's hired driver.

They are waved through. The license is stored by digital

video, and automatically logged by the guardstation computer.

CUT TO LATER, AT THE PARTY. Lenny is working the room.

It is a beautiful old Spanish, with a vaulted ceiling. The crowd is LA entertainment mid-level, agents, lawyers, junior executives. A few creatives sprinkled through, as seasoning.
This is prime turf for Lenny.
He is like the coke dealer of the early eighties. The backdoor man, chicly dangerous.

We see him working from the OUTSIDE through the tall windows. Mace is in the courtyard with the car, having a cigarette with the other drivers. She watches Lenny through the glass. He didn't invite her in. She knows he is a pretender in that glittery world, an outsider, a street guy like her . . . trying to rub up against a world that is not really his.

She is his Sancho Panza, somehow loyal despite her best instincts. It may occur to us for the first time that Mace secretly wishes Lenny would for once notice that she is a woman. But she is too cool to ever say anything. If he can't figure that one out for himself, forget it.

INSIDE, LENNY is talking to a society deb named JUDE PAIGE. She is a trust-fund baby, daughter of a Beverly Hills doctor. She is going to impress her jaded friends by going out and copping some tapes from Lenny.

SITTING IN HER CAR, Mace is talking to her younger sister by cellular. CECILE is babysitting Zander at Mace's house and wants to get going. Mace says she'll be home as soon as she can. While she's talking Mace flips open Lenny's

Haliburton, which is on the seat next to her. She looks idly at the hand-written titles on the tapes. A couple of them say "Faith," followed by the date they were recorded. Disgusted, she throws them down and latches the case.

Lenny comes out with Jude Paige. He introduces Mace, but Jude just thinks it's odd that he's introducing his driver and doesn't even look at her. Jude walks past Mace, and gets into the backseat of the car with Lenny. Mace gives her an evil stare. Lenny opens his case and goes to work.

He knows that these prim Beverly Hills third-generation rich-bitches are all fucked up, with snakes eating snakes in their heads, and the stuff they want is pretty kinky. Power-trip sex, bondage stuff, hard action . . . and a glimpse of a world they would be too terrified to ever see for themselves . . . the world of the street.

He makes a sale and Jude goes back to the party.
Lenny tells Mace he has one more stop.
She says she has to get home.

He tells her *its on the way, more or less. Just head down-town. The Retinal Fetish. You know it?*

Yeah. Lenny, I know it. It's that slime pit Faith sings at.

Mace clenches her jaw and puts the car in gear.
As they pull onto the street, another car pulls out from the curb, up the block behind them. Steckler, still following.

ENROUTE TO THE RETINAL FETISH, Lenny puts on the trodes again.
He puts a tape marked "Faith 2/12/99" in the deck and punches it on.

IN POV we experience another moment between Faith and Lenny from almost a year before. When things were still good.

In it we see Lenny's POV of them talking. Faith is curious about the squid recording. Lenny says he wants her to try it out. He wants to see what they are like together through her eyes. We see him turn off the record deck.

TAPE RESTARTS. We see the two of them standing together, reflected in a mirror. We are Faith now.

Is it on? she says, I don't feel anything.

Lenny tells her to forget it is there.

In the mirror we see that Faith has her hair pulled back tight, and the squid array covers her head. Lenny takes a wild red wig and puts it on her, hiding the array. She laughs at the look.

He turns her to him. They begin to make love.

Lenny begins to bliss out under the electrodes.

Mace is watching him in the rear-view as he plays back the electronic memories of his true love, whom Mace can't stand. He's in love with a woman on a tape, and he doesn't even see the one that's right in front of him. Plus she knows he's hurting himself with all this playback . . . getting strung out. Caught in a loop. Frying his neurons.

Mace is pissed off, feeling used and abused. Hates being his squire. She stops the car, pulling over on a commercial street. Lenny, under the wire, doesn't notice. She walks back to his door and whips it open. Punches her finger down on the STOP button of his playback deck.

IN POV we see Faith's image fade into a burst of static.

Lenny opens his eyes, disoriented. The afterimage of Faith's face is replaced by Mace's. Lenny sees they are stopped.

> **LENNY**
> What's up?

> **MACE**
> Out of the car.

> **LENNY**
> Are you angry?

She grabs him by the lapels. Jerks him out roughly.

> **LENNY**
> Hey, careful on the jacket. This is Armani.

> **MACE**
> I've had enough of this shit. You're on foot, Lenny.

> **LENNY**
> In LA? Are you crazy?

> **MACE**
> Call a cab. I'm going home. If I can remember
> where it is, it's been so long.

Mace gets in the car and peels out . . . but Lenny runs and
plasters himself on the hood. Mace accelerates, pretending
she doesn't see him.

> **MACE**
> (*calling her dispatcher*) Six to base.

> **LENNY**
> <u>Can I come in please? I'm having a hard time hear-</u>
> <u>ing the stereo.</u>

> **DISPATCHER**
> Roger, six. You still have that client?

MACE

I'm making the drop-off right <u>now</u>.

Mace jams on the brakes suddenly, throwing Lenny off (don't worry, she's not going that fast). He scrambles up, standing in front of the car. She starts to move forward . . .

LENNY

Wait! Can we talk?

MACE

Lenny, don't try me.

LENNY

I need my case. It's still in the back.

MACE

Get it.

He quickly moves comes around the car and climbs in the back door. Lenny grabs his Haliburton but instead of getting out, he leans through the divider window, next to Mace.

LENNY

Listen, can we talk a little bit here, like two rational adults?

Mace hits a button on the dash. The privacy divider rises suddenly, pinning Lenny to the ceiling.

LENNY

That would be no.

MACE

I've had it. No more of this wirehead pervo shit in my car. You wanta jerk off your brain to some

electronic 900 number, you do it somewhere else.
But not on my watch.

LENNY

Okay, you got my attention, but this is cutting off
the circulation to my head, here. D'you mind?

She lowers the divider, releasing him. Lenny straightens his
jacket and tie. Runs a hand through his greasy hair.

LENNY

I thought we were friends.

MACE

No. See, a friendship consists of more than just one
person constantly doing favors for another person.
Lately, every time I spend time with you I feel like
I've been slimed.

LENNY

Wow. Really?

MACE

Look, Lenny, I got a kid, I got rent, I got an ex-
husband someplace who doesn't send me a dime of
support . . . I'm just trying to hold on here. And
you're always comin' along with your schemes and
your slick act . . . well I'm not gonna get sucked in
anymore—

LENNY

Okay, okay, fine, I understand. I know I've been
outta line. It's just, whenever I'm in a bind, I think
of you. Because I know I can count on you in a jam,
and that's a very rare thing . . . that kind of bond
between two people.

MACE

See! There you go running a line down on me again. Damn, can't you just shutup for once and listen?

LENNY

Macey . . . I've never seen you like this.

MACE

You used to be a great guy, Lenny, but lately you've been turning into some kinda squid-head low-life bottomfeeder . . . and you're getting strung out . . . you don't even see it. You're always broke, you just go from one sleazy score to the next. I'm not going to hang around and watch you poach your brain—

LENNY

Playback is perfectly safe—

MACE

It's not, Lenny. You know it's not.

LENNY

It's my business. It's what I do.

MACE

Fine. You want your frontal lobes to look like two runny eggs, it's fine with me. Look, I gotta get some sleep.

LENNY

You still like me, don't you? We're still buddies?

MACE

(sighing, resigned) Yeah. I don't see a way out of it.

                              LENNY
You feel better now?

                              MACE
Yeah.

                              LENNY
Macey, I know you're tired but can you drop me at
the Fetish? I'm going to miss her show.

                              MACE
Sure, Lenny. The only thing worse than a junkie is
a man in love.

Mace puts the car in gear.

CUT TO Lenny entering the pounding din of THE RETI-
NAL FETISH.

The place is a fringe hangout, a converted schmatte factory,
and it is a warren of dark rooms and corridors off of a main
dancefloor. A thundering labyrinth. Steel cage-like parti-
tions of chain-link give the place a harsh, concentration-
camp atmosphere. The music is a thundering tech-thump,
and the clientele are young and on the rough side. Techie
ravers. Cybergrunge.

There are many large video screens around, including some
large projection types, which are running a continuous mon-
tage of wild graphics and images . . . a flurry of disturbing
videos (MTV via William Burroughs).

The Fetish is a street-tech hangout, a meeting place for a lot
of digital-underground types that Lenny knows. Here you
can buy and sell illicit hardware and software, plus chemicals
for the wetware (brain).

Smart-drugs are used openly, everybody trying to turbo-charge their neurons. Jack up their neurotransmitters.

We see some of the looks that are popular in '99:

The Prole look, with Sinead O'Connor stubble heads and baggy denim work uniforms, with work boots. The buzz-cuts and pajamas give them a kind of Auschwitz-meets-Metropolis look. The girls dance with their work-shirts unbuttoned . . . nothing underneath.

The Primal look: body-paint, face-paint, in primitive designs stolen from a hundred primitive cultures, but done with Day-Glo colors.

We also see mixtures of all the stuff currently out there (kilts on men, leather jackets, bicycle pants, etc). Costume ball masks and long gloves seem popular, on men and women.

OUTSIDE, MACE is driving away when she sees a limo pull up nearby. Joey Corto, Duncan and Constance get out. Gant's goon squad, minus Wade Beemer.

Mace thinks for a second. Then she swears softly. She re-parks and goes into the club.

Lenny moves through the crowd. He sees Tick and slaps five with him as he passes. Greets a few others. This is Lenny's turf also . . . the shadow side of his upscale parties. This is the tech underground, where Lenny's street cronies bring him things.
This where he buys, deals equipment, sets up "clips" . . . wires people up to go out and forage the streets for illicit experiences.

Lenny moves on, away from the din of the main floor and down trash-littered stairs to the basement. The air is rancid.

He enters a concrete connecting corridor, stepping around a girl who is holding a guy while he pukes.

Lenny sees six members of a VIETNAMESE STREET GANG coming toward him. The leader is TRAN, who is in his early twenties and the oldest. Next to him is his 15-year-old girlfriend, CINDY MINH, aka "VITA." She is a slit-eyed stone fox, very tough. Tran is cool and relaxed. Dialed in.

Lenny greets them casually, calling them the Viet Cong. He slaps Tran's palm and they get close to talk. Tran asks if Lenny has his money? Lenny laughs and says no problem. He'll come by tomorrow afternoon. Tran gives Lenny a hard time, saying he's never going to front him any more gear, but you can see they like each other. There's no anger.

Tran is a hardware dealer. A street tech pro. He runs a stolen high-tech parts ring. Sets up Lenny's rigs. Builds special stuff for him. Tran thinks life is a surreal parade. His parents squatted in rice-paddies and got napalmed. He went to high school in Huntington Beach and watched MTV. He has no discernible value system except personal survival. And he keeps an open mind about everything.
He is a smart-drug user. He pulls out an inhaler, like an asthmatic would use, and does a snort of vasopressin. He's into brain enhancement.

MACE SEARCHES the crowd for Lenny. Through the frenzy of dancers she sees Constance, Duncan and Corto also moving, scanning.

LENNY CLIMBS TO A LANDING overlooking the dancefloor. Through chain-link he sees the swirl of activity below. He goes to a door, and enters a tiny room crammed with electronics gear. It is the control room for all the

screens on the main floor. Sitting at the center of all the
wires and tape-decks is TEX ARCANA, a friend of Lenny's.
Tex whips around from one deck to another, his hands flying.

He is in a wheelchair, which he pivots nimbly.
Tex gives Lenny a high five as he comes in and pauses in his
veejaying to take a belt from a hip flask.

>   **LENNY**
> So, those rascals still haven't grown back yet, huh?

Tex looks under the blanket covering his lap. Passes his
hand through the air down there. Looks puzzled.

>   **TEX**
> Nope. Guess not. Any day now, though.

Lenny opens his briefcase and hands Tex a tape.
Tells him it's a present. No charge.
It's something he had made for him.
Tex pulls a squid-deck out of a drawer and sticks the tape
in.
He puts on the headset and pushes PLAY.

IN POV we are on a beach.
Early morning. We are running.
Running flat out, with the wind.
Looking down . . . we are barefoot on the wet sand.
Foaming water races up the sand and breaks around our
strong male legs.
Looking up again, to see our running companion . . . a
beautiful lithe woman in shorts and T-shirt. She laughs
and we speed up.
Seagulls flee before us, taking off in the dawn light.
An exquisite moment of pure life force.

TIGHT ON TEX'S FACE . . . as a tear leaks from the corner
of his eye. He is smiling like he is listening to beautiful
music.

He opens his eyes and stops the tape.
Tex softly thanks Lenny. We see the quiet magnificence of
Lenny's gift. Lenny always knows what everybody needs.
Then Tex remembers something.
He fishes around in the clutter and hands Lenny a sealed
manila envelope with "NERO" printed on it.

Tex says it was just sitting in here when he came in.
No idea who left it.
Lenny tears open the envelope. Inside is a squid tape. It is
completely unmarked.

Fan mail from some flounder?

Lenny shrugs and puts it in his pocket.

*I'll check it out later. I gotta get down there or I'm gonna
miss Faith's set.*

LENNY GOES BACK DOWNSTAIRS, and is moving down
another smoky corridor when he runs into Mace. She tells
him that Corto and Gant's goons are here.

You came back to tell me that?

I didn't want you tripping on the stairs again.

Lenny grins. Busted. He thanks her. They move through the
strobing din.
It becomes a kind of tour of Hell.
They pass people doing playback.
Lenny shows her a side room, an unfurnished room with

crumbling concrete walls where emaciated ravers are jacking-in directly to each other.
They use cheap Korean squid equipment to make a real-time hookup. Real overload stuff. Nailing the pleasure centers directly. Very unhealthy.

Lenny shows her some input-junkies sprawled in a corner.
Using low-grade gear to run orgasm-loops. Dangerous. Very addictive.
They are immobilized, jerking spasmodically.
These are true wireheads. Lost in blissed-out electronic purgatory.

Lenny thinks of this as a demonstration to Mace that what he does is a class act by comparison to these . . . the real junkies.
He doesn't get it that it's all the same thing.

This place is a kind of crossroads for all the low-life types . . .
A girl named NINA comes up to him. She is young, with a greyhound body, but her eyes are old, hiding in black pits under her hair.

Got any work for me, Lenny?

He looks at her arms . . . bruised at the elbows. Looks into her jittery eyes.

Your pupils are really slammed down . . . you slamming again? Sorry Nina, call me when you're cleaned up.

THEY MOVE ON, crossing the main floor toward the stage.
Lenny asks Mace if she knows that guy.
She turns and looks at a face in the crowd, watching them.
It is Spreg. He looks away, casually.

No. Don't know him.

*He's been watching me. And I think I saw him earlier some-
where tonight.*

THE STAGE LIGHTS COME UP suddenly and Faith is
standing there.
Like she beamed in. She is wearing a revealing leather outfit, showing a lot of her milk-white skin. Her black hair
frames her eyes, giving her an intense feral look.

The band kicks down with a wall of thundering sound.
Faith explodes into motion.
It is stunning. Her body convulses like a 440-volt mainline is
hooked up to her. She wheels across the stage, slashing her
head up and down so that her hair bursts in the strobe-
flashes like flak.

Lenny is mesmerized. He has seen this before, many times.
But it always has the same effect on him. He is transported
into another world by her, a world in which there is only the
two of them, and she dances just for him.

Faith starts to sing. It is just an inchoate wail at first, a police siren of a voice which descends through all the registers
to a fearsome growl, and then back up . . . into notes of un-
earthly beauty.

She is really good.
A techno-erotic pagan.
She seems like a force of nature.

Maybe for the first time we see in her what Lenny sees . . .
her energy, her talent, the life force flowing strong through
her like a river. Her movements are fierce and unchoreo-

graphed, exploding toward the audience and then folding in, as if wrapping around some deep inner pain.

The song is pure edge, dark, tortured.
A song of pain and loss in a speed-metal/industrial concussive rhythm.
It is scary that such anger and hurt could explode out of such a porcelain perfect face. The pain and rage of an entire tormented, hellbent planet raised to heaven in one voice.

TIGHT ON MACE, her mouth open. She's never seen Faith perform.
Holy shit. This ain't no Whitney Houston.

Faith doesn't play to the audience, or engage them in any way. She is merely taking what's in her head and letting it out. She could give a shit if they are there or not.
Faith . . . now the whirling dervish, spinning to the speed-run of the lead guitar break. Now shrieking into the silence after a climactic downbeat, and holding the note . . . holding it longer than you believe she possibly could. Then nothing.
When it is over she just drops the microphone and walks away.
Fuck you.

CUT TO LENNY and Mace entering the rat-warren of corridors backstage. Lenny tells Mace to keep an eye on the goon squad while he tries to find Faith on her break between sets.

LENNY MAKES HIS WAY to an unmarked door and goes in.
Faith is inside. It is not much of a dressing room. A cracked mirror and a bunch of boxes of cleaning supplies filling half the room.

Faith is drenched with sweat. Spent. She is kicked back, chugging a beer.
She drains it and looks at Lenny. This is the first time they have been alone together in real-time for many months.
There is so much history between them, unspoken . . . held captive in this moment. Pain and the memory of joy.

Hi, baby. I've missed you, he says.

Faith breaks the moment. She turns away. Shakes her hair and sweat flies.
She grabs a towel and asks him what was so important that he needed to talk to her about.

He says he wanted to ask her if anything was going on. If there was anything wrong.

She doesn't know what he is talking about. She says this is just another one of his ploys to get back next to her.
Faith turns to him.

> **FAITH**
> It's over, Lenny. We've been all through this. What's the point. You gotta get on with your life.

> **LENNY**
> Yeah, I know. But you didn't answer my question. Is anything wrong?

> **FAITH**
> No.

> **LENNY**
> So why would Iris tell me you might be in danger if—

FAITH

You talked to Iris?

LENNY

Yeah. But she split before she could say what was up. So what's up?

FAITH

Nothing. Iris and I don't hang out anymore. I haven't seen her in months. So who knows what's going on in her head?

LENNY

I ain't buying it. You wouldn't have called me back, had me come down here, if you didn't want to tell me something.

FAITH

I just . . . I wanted to tell you to stay away from me. Philo's acting crazy. Totally paranoid. Having his guys watching me all the time. He even hired a P.I. to follow me . . . your pal Max.

LENNY

You're kidding.

FAITH

No, it's true. That was about a month ago. But now it's . . . worse.

LENNY

Look if you're afraid of Philo, cut him loose. Pack your bags and get out.

FAITH

No, I can't.

LENNY

Why?

FAITH

If I leave now I lose everything. I've worked too
hard, Lenny. And it's finally starting to go . . . after
all the scroungy club dates and bullshit and . . . and
eating out of Styrofoam for weeks at a time, it's
going. It's happening. The video's running, and we
start the new album in a coupla weeks . . . Philo's
got it all set up—

LENNY

Fuck Philo! It's you that's up there on the stage,
not him. And it was me that got you your first club
date . . . remember? Back when we were both
starving—

FAITH

I know, Lenny. You used to make all your friends
come so the crowd would be bigger.

LENNY

Faith, I watched you create yourself out of nothing. You're like a goddamn cruise missile, targeted
on making it. And you will.

FAITH

Damn right.

LENNY

And you don't need this guy to do it. Get out. Now.
Tonight.

FAITH

No. Uh unh. I'm not gonna just run away. This
means too much to me.

LENNY

So you're gonna stay with a guy that you don't love, that you're afraid of—

FAITH

Lenny, I'm not afraid of him, it's you that should be afraid of him. You're gonna get hurt. That's what I'm trying to tell you. Just give up this quest of yours . . . give up on me.

LENNY

Can't do it.

FAITH

Give up on me, Lenny. I don't love you.

LENNY

I don't believe that.

FAITH

Go. Please. I have to go on in a couple minutes. I just need to be alone.

Lenny leaves her. When the door is closed, she stares after him. She seems about to cry, holding herself back. We see that whatever is going on in her head now, and whatever game she is running, she did love him.

In the corridor Lenny shoulders his way past some rowdy members of her band and some other scroungy music riff-raff.
He passes a figure hunched at a payphone.
Lenny stops and backs up.
The guy turns. It is Max.

LENNY

Heard about your new gig. When were you gonna tell me?

MAX

I was gonna tell ya. Shit. It's just a job.
I feel like shit about it.

LENNY

You should feel like shit.

MAX

Yeah, well you introduced me to Gant yourself, for
chrissakes, at that party . . . which one was it?

LENNY

One of 'em. Yeah. That's nothing . . . I introduced
Faith to him too.

MAX

A questionable move, given the historical perspective. Look, this gig surveilling her . . . I figured I
could take some of the prick's money, and make
sure she was okay at the same time. Do us both
some good.

LENNY

And? Is she okay?

MAX

I don't know man. This guy's a complete control
freak. And he treats her like a piece of trash. It's
not what you'd call a healthy relationship. I think
she's got a self-image problem, you ask me.

LENNY

So that mail-order psychology degree finally came,
huh?

Lenny's cellular rings and he answers it. Mace tells him

she's on the main floor but she's lost track of Philo's goons. They could be headed his way.

Lenny tells Max he's got to go. He tells Max to stay on Faith, because something might be going on. Lenny says he'll call him later.

CUT TO MACE moving through the crowd. Frenzied bodies. No sign of Corto, Constance and Duncan.

CUT TO LENNY coming down the back stairs. He rounds the corner at the bottom and . . . OH OH. Joey Corto, Constance and Duncan are right there, coming the other way.

They grab him and take him into a dank basement room. It is a large dark space, with rusted support columns and years of accumulated junk. Constance has Lenny's arm twisted painfully behind him. He can't break free.

Lenny, though he knows it's hopeless, starts his routine. He's getting to the part where he writes them all a big check when Constance slams his back up against a column and gut-punches him.
Lenny struggles but he is no match for Constance's strength and fighting skill. She works him expertly, with a series of painful jabs.
He deflates and sags to his knees.
Corto laughs. He gets a charge out of Lenny getting the shit kicked out of him by a girl.

Constance grabs him by his hair and pulls him up with one powerful arm. She is cocking back the other arm for a pile-driver punch when . . .

Suddenly a dark shape materializes behind her.
Mace drives Constance head first into the steel column.

Duncan lunges in and grabs for Mace.

This is a mistake.

Mace doesn't fight fancy. And she doesn't fight fair.

She fights to win. And she is awesomely fast.

Her moves are street moves, coupled with arm-locks and come-alongs she has been trained to use as a security driver.

Lenny recovers enough to get some licks in on Constance, who is still a little stunned. She has blood dripping in her eyes and can't see too well. He calls her a Hell Dyke and gets her to charge, then breaks a dusty old chair over her head.

Mace drops Duncan about the time Constance is hitting the ground, leaving . . .

Joey Corto, who fumbles out a Beretta 9mm and sticks it in Mace's face.

He sniggers, loving the upper hand.

Safety's on, she says. So, like a jerk, he looks.

She snaps sideways in a headfake and closes blindingly fast, twisting the gun out of his hand. She continues to twist his wrist brutally and Corto goes down to one knee, groaning.

She takes his Beretta and backhands the barrel hard across his face.

Mace releases his wrist and he crumples in a heap.

She and Lenny back out the door.

Then Lenny runs back in and kicks Corto in the ribs.

Lenny! Mace grabs him and pulls him out of the room, then slams the heavy metal firedoor behind them. She locks it with a piece of junk wedged behind the release bar.

They walk quickly along the corridor to an exit into the alley behind the club. Mace is disassembling Corto's Beretta without looking at it as they walk. She drops pieces in dumpsters as they go.

Lenny brushes himself off and checks his jacket for damage. Mentions how the fabric is really great. Never takes a wrinkle. It is a metaphor for him. He keeps getting folded the wrong way and manages to bounce back. Teflon. Nothing sticks.

Mace asks him if he ever wondered why he gets beat up a lot.
He never really thought about it.
She offers him a ride home.

LENNY AND MACE ON THE DRIVE TO HIS PLACE. They are relaxed and easy. She offers him a belt from her tiny hip flask.

> **MACE**
> Lenny Nero. You're some piece of work. You just calmly backstroking around in the big toilet bowl, and somehow you never let it touch you. Like some kinda Teflon man.

> **LENNY**
> Thank you.

> **MACE**
> I mean, the man's seen it all, right? Between working Vice and your current so-called occupation, you must've seen every kinda perversion.

> **LENNY**
> Every dark need. Every wrinkle in the human brain. I have crawled through the gutter of sexual dysfunction.

MACE
What I'm sayin'. But you still manage to be this
goofball romantic. What is that, some kinda de-
fense mechanism?

LENNY
It is my sword and my shield, Macey.

Lenny finds the anonymous tape in his pocket.
He looks at it, puzzled.
Mace asks what it is. He says he has no idea.
He opens his briefcase. Pops it into the deck.
Settles the trodes on his head.
He punches PLAY and closes his eyes.

**POV SEQUENCE: This will be intercut between the ac-
tual POV and Lenny's reactions as he mentions some of
what he is experiencing to Mace, sitting next to him.**

**The first thing we notice is that the POV is distorted vi-
sually. The colors are de-saturated. Almost black and
white. Yet the detail is crisp and clear, almost hyper-real.**

**WE ARE WALKING down a hallway at a large hotel. An
apparently endless row of doors. No sense of whether it
is night or day.**
**The Wearer's glance goes to the numbers on the doors
from time to time. We come to a particular door. There
is a DO NOT DISTURB sign on the door. The Wearer
moves to the room next door.**
Looks both ways. The corridor is empty.

It's a test-pattern so far. Lenny says.

"Our" hands appear, quickly pulling on latex surgical

gloves. They look like male hands. The snapping of the
rubber is the only sound in the corridor.
The POV hunches down to the lock and we see the hands
go to work with lock-picking tools. Several seconds and
the lock is very professionally picked.

Okay, we got a little B and E action now, Lenny says to
Mace.

We enter the dark room, which is vacant.
The drapes are open and we see city lights. It is night.
One gloved hand picks up the guest directory and looks
at it in the moonlight coming in the window.
The SUNSET REGENT.

The Wearer drops the directory and the hands reappear
holding . . . a black ski-mask. He pulls it on, leaving the
subsequent POV seen through the eye-holes of the mask.
The Wearer now looks up into a mirror on the dresser.
He has avoided his reflection up until now. We see a man,
dressed in a jogging suit and black fanny-pack, and of
course the ski-mask. Totally anonymous.

Hey, this is getting interesting, Lenny says. *This guy is
good with the suspense.*

The wearer crosses to the balcony door. Opens it quietly
and goes outside, moving to the wall dividing this room's
balcony from the one next door.

The Wearer climbs the railing and, six stories above the
pavement, slips around the wall, stepping down onto
the other balcony. We hug the wall, looking furtively into
the room. It is a suite. In the living room we see a woman
making herself a drink at the mini-bar.
She turns . . .

It is Iris.
She is wearing a T-shirt and panties. Probably ready for
bed. She looks like she can't sleep. Pours the Scotch
shakily.

CUT TO LENNY, the streetlights washing across his face.
He gets suddenly serious with a flash of premonitory dread.

IN POV we see Iris go into the bedroom, out of sight. We
can hear the television on in there. Using a steel jimmy
the Wearer slips the latch on the balcony slider and si-
lently opens it, slipping inside.
We stalk quietly to the bedroom door, listening to her
movements.
Water running in the bathroom.
We come around the doorframe.
Bedroom dark, bathed in TV glow.
Iris in the bathroom, washing her face with cold water.

We move toward her.
Crossing the room as she reaches for a towel.
We are now only a couple of feet away.
She comes out of the bathroom, walking right past us,
drying her face.
She lowers the towel, turning away . . . her eyes whip
back.
Widening in terror.
She reacts with surprising speed, diving across the bed.
We go after her.

Her hand goes under the pillow and comes out with a
small automatic pistol. She whips it around toward us
but we grab it before she can fire and twist it away.
She smashes the palm of her hand into our face and rolls
off the bed.
All this happens lightning-fast.

We follow her as she scrambles up, running through the bedroom door.

Across the living room and down the short hall to the front door.

Closing rapidly on her as she somehow gets the chain off the door and gets out into the hall.

Slam! We tackle her against the far wall of the corridor.

Our right hand comes into view holding a small electric stunner.

Zap! We nail her right in the back, between the shoulder blades.

She sags to the floor, gasping. We zap her again.

The Wearer's glance does a 180 both ways down the corridor . . . nobody in sight.

We clamp our hand over Iris' mouth and drag her back into her room, locking the door.

ON LENNY, reacting. Going white. *What is it?* Mace says.

WE ARE DRAGGING a semiconscious Iris into the bathroom . . . propping her up with her back against the white tile wall . . . grabbing her hands and handcuffing them one by one to the steel towel rack above her.

She is moaning, stunned. Crying now.

I don't have it, she says, then something else we can't quite make out. She is hardly able to draw a breath to talk, let alone scream.

I haven't seen your face . . . I haven't heard your voice . . . you can still let me go—

ZAP! The Wearer hits her with the stunner again. She jerks and gasps for breath. We see our latex-gloved finger come up in front of us and hear SSSHHH.

Moving quickly now. Our hands unbuckle the fanny pack and lay it on the floor next to her. Unzip it. Pull out something . . . a set of playback trodes. Our hands place them on her head. She stares uncomprehending. What?

We catch a glimpse of some electronics stuff inside the pack . . . a record deck, some wires, a small metal box.

What's he doing? He's jacked her in to his own output, Lenny says, *She's seeing what he's seeing. She's seeing herself.*

Iris can now see herself as the Wearer sees her . . . wide-eyed with terror, white-lipped, weeping. Helpless. And she can feel what he feels.
The Wearer's hand goes back into the fanny-pack and pulls out something else. A black athletic headband. We slip it over her head, down over her eyes. A blindfold. Now she can only see what the wearer sees.
And also from the bag we pull . . .
A yellow plastic object. With our thumb we extend the five inch blade of the razor knife. It is the type with the tips that can be broken off by segments when they get dull. It extends with an ominous clicking sound.

We lower it toward her and cut up the middle of her T-shirt, laying it open. Exposing her torso. We then look down and slide the knife under the side band of her panties, slicing them off.
We put the knife up to her throat, and she whimpers, afraid to cry out, and then we draw the flat side of the blade down across her body as if to tease her with the prospect of her death.
Lenny is feeling the stalker's exhilaration, pounding heart, flushed skin, panting breath, and Lenny knows that Iris is feeling the same thing, overlaid with her own

senses . . . so the excitement and terror merge into one thing, one overwhelming wave of dread sensation.

MACE LOOKS AT LENNY'S EXPRESSION of dawning horror and pulls the car to the curb. It is a commercial street, with rows of closed stores. Nobody around.
Lenny is hyperventilating, shifting in his seat as if ants are crawling over him.

IN POV we see the Wearer pull his jogging pants down below his knees (R-rated please) and reach for Iris. Kneeling in front of her, he pushes her legs apart and pulls her hips forward onto him. Though it is below frame, we can tell that he is pushing into her.
Iris is feeling and seeing what he sees and feels . . .
She feels what the attacker feels as he slides inside her, her pain and humiliation swirling with the killer's exhilaration.

ON LENNY, sweating and barely able to breathe.
Mace stops the tape . . . concerned by Lenny's reaction. He opens his eyes . . . Mace sees the fear there, of what the tape may reveal. She knows something really serious is going down on the recording. Lenny can't describe it. But he has to go on. He has to know.
He pushes her hand away and punches PLAY.

IT FLOODS INTO HIS HEAD AGAIN. The sweaty, grunting horror.
The stalker picks up her slit T-shirt and quickly wraps it around her neck. He knots it tight and twists one powerful hand into the knot. The muscles in his forearm look like cables as he turns the knot tighter.
As the stalker is about to come he viciously twists the knot a full turn and the T-shirt fabric almost disappears into the skin under her jaw.

Via her trodes, Iris watches herself die.
Her death comes at the moment of his orgasm which is
fed to her . . . the two most powerful and profound mo-
ments in life, essential opposites, fusing into one thing
. . . blasting off the planet on total overload . . . terror,
pain, death merging with ecstasy and exhultation at the
same instant.

ON LENNY, crying out and grabbing for the trodes, but he
just holds onto them, as if they are sucking his brains out of
his skull.
Oh my God, is all he can say, over and over like a mantra.

BACK TO POV, a glimpse of the Wearer's hand relaxing
the knot. Iris' head lolls. Her mouth is slack and open.
We remove her blindfold. Her eyes are half-lidded. Very
dead looking. Our fingers gently push them wide open.

BACK TO LENNY, looking like he has been gut kicked. He
gasps for breath.

TO POV, as the killer's hand calmly moves Iris's head
from side to side . . . studying her dead face. Her staring
eyes. The killer's hands form a frame with thumbs and
forefingers . . . he is framing her face with his hands like
a director lining up a closeup.
He leans very close to her and stares into one dead eye,
the pupil wide, seeing nothing.
A burst of static. End of tape.

Lenny opens his eyes. He fumbles open the car door and
practically rolls out onto the sidewalk. The trodes pull off
his head as he lurches up, reeling across the sidewalk to a
darkened storefront where he leans for support. He doubles
over and heaves up the contents of his stomach.

Mace circles around the car and catches him as he sags to his knees.

She holds his shoulders while he throws up again.

Lenny tries to tell her what he just experienced, but he can barely find the words.

He tells her it is a snuff clip . . . a black-jack.

It is the worst he has ever experienced. And the madness . . . of wanting to show the victim her own death, while recording that reaction . . . and then the further madness of giving the tape to him, like a little present, sharing that horrible intimacy of rape and murder with another . . . so sick, so psychotically scopophilic.

Lenny is shocked to his soul. This would be the worst thing he had ever seen and felt even if it wasn't someone he knew.

Are you sure it's real? she asks.

Yeah. He's sure. He's seen some that were faked. But you can tell. This one had no cuts. No way to hide the blood tubes and stuff.

This was real.

Lenny gets up and says they have to go to the hotel.

It's only a couple of minutes away from where they are.

They pull up to the hotel and there are cops everywhere and they are just loading Iris into the coroner's van.

Drive on, Lenny says.

He calls Max via cellular, catching him still at the Retinal Fetish. Max says Faith just left with Gant's goons and he's off for the night. Lenny tells him to meet him at his house ASAP.

CUT TO the three of them at Lenny's apartment.

Max, the hardened homicide detective, is removing the trodes with shaky hands. His face is gray. He doesn't say a word. He grabs the tequilla bottle from the table in front of him and takes a long chug.

That is one sick fuck, he finally says.

He offers the playback trodes to Mace who declines.
Lenny is still shaken by what he experienced on the tape.
On top of which he feels guilty.
Iris had come to him for help. And he had shined her on. He should have read it better. Known something was wrong. But at the time she just seemed like another strung-out hooker having a bad night.

But . . . it's like she knew she was going to die.

Max and Lenny have seen plenty of what the city has had to offer over the years in the way of sickness and death. They start to let the professional cop reflexes take over . . . to analyze the killing.

Max comments on the twisted idea of showing the girl her own death through the killer's eyes using the squid deck and some kind of real-time hookup. Lenny says yeah, he must have been using some kind of splitter box, sending the signal to the recorder and to her at the same time.

This guy is really damaged goods, Max says.

Or that's what he wants us to think, Lenny says.
Lenny thinks maybe the guy wants to make it look like he is some kind of psychotic sex killer . . . a psycho john . . . which explains why there was no attempt to dispose of the body and clean up.
It would be important that Iris be found as she was killed, handcuffed, with sperm at the scene, etc. Forensics will conclude it was a trick gone wrong, she is a known call-girl . . .

they will write it off quickly. Hookers are always getting whacked by psychos and serial killers. The cops give up fast on cases like this because the usual process of getting information on the street doesn't work, these guys act alone . . . and anyway society at large doesn't give a rat's ass about a dead hooker.

Max says, *Yeah, it's all about what it looks like when you walk into the scene. The homicide guys will see a sex killer, they won't look beyond that, because that's what the scene says to them. They walk in . . . you got a dead hooker, handcuffs, semen present . . . they know they'll never find the guy.*

Max and Lenny go through the crime scene, what happens in the tape, etc.
Max says, *It could go either way . . . a true sex killer, or somebody who knows enough about it and is cold-blooded enough to make it look that way, to disguise the crime which actually has another purpose . . . like to shut Iris up. Maybe this guy's not crazy at all. Just wants us to think he is.*

Mace says, *Wait a minute, here. This guy might have some kind of real motive, but if he could think of what's on that tape, and go through with it, then he's still a raving fucking psychotic.*

Okay, fine, Lenny says pacing, *he's a psychotic who thinks he's sane pretending to be a psychotic. But what's going on here? Why was Iris at the hotel? Was she meeting a regular or was she hiding out? And what was it she was trying to tell me earlier?*
And why would the killer give the tape to me?

Mace lists what they know:
Iris is raped and killed the same night she comes to Lenny

for help. She appears paranoid and says that Faith is in danger.

She later is at a hotel, possibly in hiding, but the killer knows where she is.

And the killer knows Lenny, and knows where to find him, to get him the tape. And the killer knows how to use squid recorders and playback equipment.

Lenny says he knows about a hundred people that fit that description. That's the problem, Max says, Lenny knows everybody. And if it has something to do with squid recording, sooner or later it washes up on Lenny's beach. 'Cause Lenny's the man. The Magic Man.

Maybe the tape was given to Lenny so it would get copied and distributed . . . the guy doesn't know Lenny doesn't deal in that stuff . . . figures it could become some kind of snuff top-ten hit. A kind of bragging. Sharing with other sick fucks.

Or maybe it's a message to Lenny, Mace says. But what?

Lenny tells Max he thinks he's being followed.

Max dismisses it.

Says Lenny is always paranoid. That's what comes from being in the watching game. After a while you're convinced someone is always watching you.

Lenny is primarily concerned with what the connection might be to Faith. He's afraid for her. Faith and Iris have been friends for years. Lenny met them on the street back in his Vice days, when Faith was just another runaway. The usual teen tragedy.

And recently Iris has done the occasional clip for Lenny. Meatwork. Nothing too kinky. She was off the streets, working out of her apartment in Silver Lake, trying to build a reputation as a classier act. Faith sort of cut her off when the music thing started to happen. Didn't want the connection. But Iris was always loyal to Faith. Admired her from afar. Someone from the street that was making it.

Mace says they have to get the tape to the cops.
Lenny says no . . . he wants to study it. Those bozos wouldn't know what to do with it.
Yeah, that's best, Max says. *If Lenny calls the cops, he'll get busted for possession of illegal electronics gear. A third offense. Definite jail time. Anyway, I know all those guys, so I can find out if they come up with anything . . . I'll just tell them she was a friend of mine and they'll keep me in the loop. Get me the forensics reports and all that.*

Max leaves.
Lenny calls Faith. We see the phone ringing in Philo Gant's luxurious house in the Hollywood Hills. A total contrast to Lenny's ratty digs. Joey Corto answers the phone. He has stitches on the bridge of his nose, which looks broken.
Lenny asks to speak to Faith. Says it's her brother.

Corto calls to Faith, who is in the kitchen. She crosses the living room, looking out of place. She is still wearing her outfit from the gig earlier, and it contrasts with the polished marble and glass of Gant's house. There is a fire burning in the fireplace, and its light flickers over all the glossy surfaces.
Faith answers the phone.

Lenny tells her that Iris is dead.
She is shocked. What happened? she says.

CUT TO PHILO GANT, listening on another line. He is in his den, watching Faith on one of many video surveillance monitors. Philo does like to watch.

Lenny is asking Faith if she knows why Iris was staying at the hotel instead of her apartment when Philo appears next to Faith.

He takes the phone from her and tells Lenny it's past his bedtime.

Hangs up.

Faith tells him that Iris was murdered.

Gant's expression is hard to read. He doesn't seem surprised.

Faith makes an intuitive leap. She says, *You already knew, didn't you? What the fuck is going on?*

He tells her to quit being so paranoid. Of course he didn't know. And she better stay the fuck away from Nero.

An argument erupts. We see that Gant is unstable, trembling with pent-up rage. Or is it fear?

He sweeps all the glasses off the bar.

They shatter on the polished marble floor.

She says she will talk to or see anyone she wants, anytime she wants.

He slaps her hard, without warning.

She falls to the floor, amid the broken glass.

Gant walks out.

Faith is left in the elegant living room, surrounded by black marble and glass, with the lights of the city below. She has come far from the street. She is living in the dream she imagined for herself, but it has become a nightmare. Gasping for breath, she picks herself up and slowly crosses the beautiful room.

CUT TO LENNY under the wire. He is playing back the

tape of Iris's death. Mace is watching him, making notes when he says something.

He stops the tape suddenly and rewinds, playing back a section again.

Talking to himself . . . to the killer inside his head.

In POV the killer enters the vacant hotel room. He passes the mirror on the dresser.

Lenny plays it back again . . . trying to will the killer to turn.

You know there's a mirror right there and you're keeping your eyes off it, you fuck. You know what you're doing. You've worn before. Who are you?

He goes back and forth, back and forth, through different sections. Mace paces nervously, watching him. She can't stand to watch him burn his brain like this.

Lenny pulls the back off the record deck and uses a black-box amplifier to boost the gain. The signal is now stronger. Clearer.

More like he is there. He can feel more. He is inside the killer's head.

This is dangerous shit. The playback equivalent of speed-balling.

With the boosted gain he is overloading his own cerebral cortex with sensation . . . hoping for a clue, a revelation. Trying to push through the veil of identity.

He runs the death-tape again, barely able to talk, straining like he's lifting a grand piano. Mace finally can't stand it anymore and jerks the trodes off his head.

Lenny gives up. He sags back on the couch.

He rubs his eyes. He is seeing ghosts, afterimages burned

into his visual cortex. The room is alive with them. Iris' terrified face floating iridescent on his living room wall.
The whole room seems to shimmer.

You okay? Mace asks him.

Starting to get the jaggies, here.

He tries to stand, but he is unsteady.
Mace helps him to the kitchen sink where he runs cold water
over his head. He washes four Tylenol down with a shot of
tequilla.

CUT TO LATER. Lenny is collapsed on the couch.
His head is in Mace's lap.
He is deeply asleep. She looks down at him, gently brushes
his hair off his sweaty forehead in an unconsciously maternal
gesture.
Mace gazes at Lenny's sleeping face. She has an unexpected
moment of realization . . . somehow, improbably, she loves
him.
Mace sighs and leans her head back against the wall.
Go figure.

CUT TO MACE pulling her limo into the driveway of a mod-
est stucco house in Inglewood. It is dawn. Her neighbor is
walking the dog.
She goes inside.
CECILE, her younger sister, is still asleep on the couch,
wearing her clothes. ZANDER, her five-year-old, is up
watching TV in his pajamas, eating Cheerios. She goes to
him and hugs him.
You got to stop pulling these allnighters, Mom, he says.

2:20 PM, December 31

Lenny wakes up to the sound of the phone ringing.
He is on the couch, still clothed. He hears Max's voice on
the answer machine and grabs the phone, his head obviously
pounding. His *jaggies* have faded, leaving only the headache.

Max tells him that he did some checking at the station and
Iris checked in under a false name. She paid cash. Said she
was staying a couple of days. Looks like she was hiding out.
The cops don't have any real leads. Nobody saw or heard
anything.

Where's Faith? Lenny says.
She hasn't left Gant's house yet today, Max says. He's in his
car, staking out the house from up the block.
Stick to her, Lenny tells him.

As he is hanging up he notices something.
A manila envelope stuck between the steel bars and the
glass of his front window, next to the door.
"NERO" is printed on the envelope.

Oh shit.
He opens the door, looking both ways. No one is around.
He fishes out the envelope from behind the bars and takes it
inside.
Of course it contains a tape. He stares at it with dread.

Lenny sits down and puts the tape in his playback deck.
He picks up the trodes and places them on his head. He notices his hands are shaking. He takes a deep breath and
punches PLAY.

POV SEQUENCE: DAY. As expected we see the de-saturated signature of the killer's vision. The Wearer is walking through the courtyard of Lenny's apartment building. We recognize it by the unkempt pool, the sunken deck furniture. We walk through a breezeway to an alley-like courtyard behind the building. We approach a door . . . the back door to Lenny's apartment.

The killer picks the lock on the back door. Opens the door and enters. The apartment is dark, blacked out. We are in the kitchen. We stop and listen. Water dripping in the sink. Soft snoring from the living room.

Moving to the other room. Slowly, silently. Furtively looking around the doorframe to the living room. There is Lenny, crashed out on the couch, sawing logs.

Now moving stealthily toward him. Kneeling down beside him. Lenny, burned out from the night before, is deep under. Our hands come into view, holding the yellow plastic razor knife. With his thumb, the killer extends the blade . . . click, click, click, click. Lenny snores on.
The blade flashes in a beam of sunlight as it moves toward Lenny.
The killer lays it gently against Lenny's throat. Draws it slowly across . . . not leaving a mark.
The POV backs away and—
Static as the tape ends.

LENNY, IN THE PRESENT, whips off the trodes, freaking.
He feels around his throat with one hand . . . can't feel anything.
Crossing quickly to a mirror near the front door, he inspects

his neck minutely. There is a hair-fine red line over his carotid.

He looks around the room wildly, his heart hammering.

Slowly, he gets his breathing under control.

Fuck, he says in a long slow exhalation.

Then . . . he hears something in the kitchen. A tiny click.

His eyes go wide. Hyperventilating, Lenny moves quickly to a cardboard box full of junk. He fishes around in it, under a bunch of papers and junk, and pulls out a GLOCK 23 .45 auto pistol.

He stalks silently toward the kitchen.

Then he looks at the butt of the pistol-grip and sees there is no magazine.

He un-stalks back to the box and finds a loaded magazine under a bunch of unpaid bills. He inserts it quietly, wincing as he chambers a round. It clicks as it feeds in.

Heart thudding, he works his way to the kitchen door.

He edges around the frame, pie-ing the room, pistol at the low-ready position.

Mace is sitting at the kitchen table, giving him a funny look. She is drinking a cup of coffee, made from the jar of instant on the counter. She is dressed casually in bicycle pants, work boots and oversized nylon jacket over a tank-top.

W'sup Lenny?

He deflates, lowering the gun. His hands are shaking.

Jesus, Mace!

I knocked but there was no answer, she says. *The back door was open so I came in and saw you were under the wire, so I made coffee. You look bad. What's going on?*

CUT TO Lenny throwing stuff into a folding bag. He is wired on adrenaline. He tells Mace not to talk . . . the place could be under audio surveillance. He is really cranked on paranoia. He grabs some clothes, and a box of .45 hollow points. He puts them in the bag along with a playback deck. He asks Mace to hand him his shoebox full of Faith tapes. She hands it to him with distaste.

Lenny is about to zip the bag when he decides he doesn't like the tie for the jacket he's picked. Goes back to the bedroom and switches it. Even fleeing for his life there are certain lines he won't cross.

Last, Lenny grabs his grimy old Second-chance body armor from the LAPD days and stuffs it into his Haliburton.

IN MACE'S CAR, Lenny keeps looking behind them. Mace tells him they're not being followed. Lenny can't relax.

What is the killer trying to do?

It's like he's taunting him, or trying to get him to do something.

But what?

We hear the car radio, more New Year's Eve hype.

Lenny is oblivious to it. He is also oblivious to the low-rent neighborhood they have entered.

Outside the car, we see increasing evidence of past and present street warfare. Burned out buildings in a long row, gang-tag graffiti everywhere, tough looking guys riding around in cars, wearing bandanas and giving the limo the evil eye.

There are cops in body armor and helmets on some street-corners, holding automatic rifles. Helicopters orbit endlessly. Several blocks away, a column of smoke blackens the sky from some isolated eruption of violence or arson.

They pass through a police checkpoint.

Cops have a car pulled out of the line, and are shaking down

the occupants for weapons. Three Hispanic guys are standing around with their hands on their heads, looking pissed
off as the cops do the "routine search."
We realize that LA's approach to crime has been to slide
slowly toward a police-state. We should get the feeling from
this driving sequence that the city is living almost in a state
of siege, ready to erupt into chaos and rioting with very little
provocation.
Mace says the death of Jeriko One has got things stirred up,
so the cops are beefing up their presence on the street. The
LAPD says Jeriko got done by 36th Street, because their
tags were at the scene. But 36th Street says they didn't do
it.

They arrive at Mace's house. By daylight, we see that she
lives on a lower income street, in a mostly black neighborhood.
Lenny throws his stuff down in the living room and goes
with Mace out to the tiny backyard. Cecile is there, hanging
out with her boyfriend, CURTIS, and Curtis' friend VEJ.
These two guys are about 18, dressed in gangsta garb, bandanas on their heads.
They are listening to "The Prophets of Light" on a CD
player.
They stare at Lenny like he is from Mars.

Zander runs up to Lenny with his arms out, and Lenny
hoists him over his head. Lenny flies him around the yard,
and then they get into a deep conversation about some eso-
teric five-year-old stuff.
Mace watches Lenny with Zander for a moment. The kid
loves him. Then she tells Cecile to stay and babysit a while
longer, because she and Lenny are going out again.
Cecile loses it over that one but Mace chills her with a look.
You don't mess with Mace.

MACE'S CAR IS CRUISING through the late afternoon
traffic.

Lenny is on the cellular to Max.
He tells him that they are going to TRAN'S to see if he can
make anything of the killer's tapes.
Max wants to meet him there but Lenny asks him to stay on
the surveillance of Faith. He's sure, somehow, that this has
something to do with her, and he needs to know that she is
safe.

A STREET IN THE WAREHOUSE DISTRICT. Mace's
car pulls up to the loading ramp of a nondescript building.
Graffiti-covered brick and broken windows.

INSIDE THE WAREHOUSE Lenny leads Mace to a massive freight elevator. He keys an intercom and says, *Yo,
Tran. It's Lenny. You up there, bud?*

His answer is the sound of the freight elevator starting up
with a clanking rumble. The open cage descends to meet
them.
Lenny rolls up the safety bars and motions to Mace to step
into the cage. He hits the button. They ascend.

IN THE ELEVATOR. As they ride up three levels, Lenny
is running a stream-of-consciousness riff on Iris' death.
The fact that she did a lot of wire-work, for a lot of different
people. Maybe she saw something, caught something on a
clip . . . something dangerous to the wrong person. And whoever wired her up is afraid those wrong people will trace the
whole thing back to them . . . could be anything, drugs,
gangs, mafia, corrupt politicians.
She could have recorded something which got her killed.

But was the killer someone Iris saw and recorded, or was it
whoever she was wearing for?

The elevator lurches to a stop and Lenny rolls up the safety
grate.

LENNY NERO is mesmerized as he watches Faith sing at the Retinal Fetish, transported into a world in which she performs just for him.

LORNETTE "MACE" MASON: Late twenties, striking features. Mace and Lenny are friends. It's not the first time Lenny has tried to bring Mace into his nocturnal underworld.

FAITH JUSTIN is a singer. A rock star wannabe, a techo-erotic pagan. She moves with a lithe, sinuous grace, the life force flowing strong through her like a river.

TICK is totally plugged into the wiretripping scene. He is a hardware dealer, a street tech pro. Tick runs a stolen high-tech parts ring.

Officers STECKLER and ENGELMAN, in plain clothes, keep Lenny and Mace under surveillance from their unmarked car.

FAITH JUSTIN and PHILO GANT, her manager/record producer.
Gant treats Faith like chattel. But they both play that game, and
get what they need out of it.

MACE kisses LENNY lightly on the forehead, consigning them to
their destinies.

MAX PELTIER, Lenny's friend, is a former cop. Max believes in the lowest and most venal interpretation of any given event. He is seldom disappointed.

FAITH explodes into motion. Her body convulses like a 400-volt mainline. Faith slashes her head up and down so that her hair flashes in the strobe lights.

LENNY's reality: high-tech lowlife.

Lenny has one last chance to change his life, to turn himself around or sink into darkness. History ends and begins again at the mother of all parties on New Year's Eve, December 31, 1999—the dawn of a new millennium.

They walk out into a dark, expansive loft. Most of the space is empty, just a dusty cavernous storage space. The windows are blacked out. At the far end is an island of light.
They walk toward it.

Under fluorescents, Tran sits at a table stacked high with exotic electronics gear. It is a sort of workshop/living space, with a couch and some chairs stuck in among racks of component electronics. There are two computer workstations, with half a dozen monitor screens. Plus lots of squid gear . . . record and playback equipment. Copy decks. Signal processing gear.
Cables snake everywhere over the floor, and there are piles of junk and boxes full of chips, chasis, and components of all types. There is a refrigerator, a microwave, and a ping-pong table piled up with mostly empty pizza boxes.
Several large-screen TVs are running, unwatched.
A true cyberpunk place.

VITA MINH is there, sitting on a table near Tran. In a lawn chair sits a VIETNAMESE GANGMEMBER with an AR-15 lying across the arms of the chair. All three of them are skinny and dangerous-looking.

Tran is working on his pet project. He wants to put squid recordings out on a pirate computer-net. He's working on a compression/encryption algorithm to allow him to send squidnet data out over a bootleg high-bandwidth fiber system to thousands of wiretrippers all over the country. He wants to be the first squidnet deejay of the neural underground.

Lenny holds up the two anonymous tapes and tells Tran to play them down.

What you got there, Lenny? Some new meatwire clips?

It's a black-jack, Tran. A bad one. I need you to look at it.

Tran shrugs. Takes a blast from his vasopressin inhaler. *Why not.*

CUT TO MINUTES LATER.
Tran seems uneffected emotionally by the tape. In fact he is revved up. He digs the performance art aspect of the piece. Vita is making faces as she plays the tape and saying *great eyefuck.*

Lenny reminds Tran that he came here for a technical analysis of the tape, not a fucking art critique.

Tran starts with the de-saturation. Says the killer has some kind of distortion of the color and gray-scale values in his visual cortex . . . a sort of color blindness. He runs the signal from the tape through his processing equipment and says, *See, look at the peak-period ratios here . . . there's something wrong with this guy. Maybe some kind of tumor, brain lesion. Some kind of trauma.*

Makes sense, Lenny says, *a lot of psycho killers have had brain injuries. What about the real-time hookup?*

He's using some kind of box to split the signal. So it goes to the recorder and directly to the trode set he put on the girl.

You ever make a box like that?

Yeah, I've sold a few. But I can't see it well enough in the clip to tell if it's one of mine. He doesn't let his eyes settle on the gear.

Yeah, I know. What about what she's saying. Can you do anything to clarify the signal? I can't make it out.

Tran goes to work. He gets the tape back from Vita and puts into his master deck. He puts on a trode set and finds the section on the tape where Iris talks. He samples it off to the computer where he processes the signal. Muttering to himself. He pops some choline and vincamine, and does another big snort from his inhaler while he works.

He gives Lenny the trodes to check out the processed signal.

IN POV we see Iris again, white faced and panting. The sound is much clearer.

She says *I don't have it . . . I gave it to somebody . . . a guy I know . . . please . . . I haven't seen your face . . . I haven't heard your voice . . . you can still let me go . . .*

Lenny takes off the trodes. Realizes "the guy" is him. But she didn't give him anything.

Mace tells Lenny to think of exactly what Iris said when she came into the bar. He remembers her saying she didn't want to come in but she changed her mind.

Mace figures maybe she put *it,* whatever *it* is, in Lenny's car. Thinking he would get it when he came out. But then the car got towed.
Lenny thinks about it, realizing she is right.
He runs out without thanking Tran.

DUSK. The last night of this millenium is falling.
AT THE IMPOUND YARD IN SAN PEDRO, Mace's car
pulls to the curb. The yard is located in the vast no-man's
land of storage lots, cranes and warehouses near the piers
of the harbor. The impound office is locked. Closed for New
Year's Eve.

Mace and Lenny get out. She goes to the trunk and opens
it. Inside are an assortment of things she brought, in case.
Shotgun, flashlights, walkie-talkies. Bolt-cutters.

CUT TO Lenny and Mace cutting the chain off the gate with
the long-handled bolt-cutters. They enter the yard. Mace is
carrying a blunt object that looks like a ray-gun. A TAZER.

Right on cue a huge Rottweiler bounds out of the shadows
at them, growling, its head low on an attack run. Mace fires
and the tazer lights up the dog with 120,000 volts (low am-
perage/not lethal). It whines and flips over twice, then runs
off behind some parked cars.

Lenny spots his BMW in the lot and they go to it. The car is
blocked in by ten other cars, so he's not getting it back this
trip.
He unlocks the door and looks inside with a tiny mag-lite
while Mace covers them with the tazer. A puppy-like whine
comes occasionally from behind some cars nearby. We catch
a glimpse of the puzzled, snuffling Rottweiler eyeing them
warily.
Lenny finds the tape on the floormat, passenger side, still

wrapped in the note. He reads the note . . . LENNY, HELP
ME. Shit. Guilt hits him all over again. He crumples the
note, puts the tape in his briefcase, and they head for the
gate. It is almost full night now.

As they reach the car they are hit by two flashlight beams.
It is the two cops, STECKLER AND ENGELMAN, out of
uniform, but looking very serious with their pistols aimed at
Lenny and Mace.
They have been following Lenny, knowing sooner or later he
would lead them to the tape.

Steckler tells Lenny to give him the tape. Lenny says it's in
his case.
At that moment the pissed-off Rottweiler shoots through the
open gate like a black torpedo and tears into Engelman's
leg.

Engelman shoots the dog.

Lenny swings up his Haliburton, using it as a shield, and
dives for the car. The case takes three rounds from
Steckler's 9mm before Lenny gets behind cover. Mace just
seems to vanish.
She reappears over the trunk of the limo and puts two
rounds squarely into Steckler's chest, knocking him down.
Lenny and Mace scramble into the car, starting it up.

Steckler sits up, pulling up his shirt to make sure his body
armor stopped the slugs. No blood. He comes up firing. He
and Engelman empty their magazines at the limo as it pulls
away.
They realize it is bulletproof and run to their pickup truck,
parked nearby, to give chase.

Steckler's face is a mask of rage. He slams the truck in gear and accelerates after the limo before Engelman even has the door closed.

Inside the limo, Mace is doing her thing . . . what she's trained for. Security driving. She whips some moves in the big car, but the truck stays behind her. It is closing on them.

Oh no, we're not being followed, Lenny. Don't be so paranoid, Lenny, he says.

Mace isn't listening. She's concentrating on driving.
Lenny has his briefcase open . . . Steckler's shots have shattered the equipment inside. He pulls out the tape they found in his car.
They hear rounds hitting the car, and look back.
The truck is right behind them.
Mace tells Lenny not to worry . . . all the glass is bullet resistant.

Bullet resistant? Whatever happened to bulletproof?!

Engelman leans out the passenger side window with an AK-47 assault rifle. He rips off several bursts which riddle the limo, cracking the glass in starburst patterns. The lexan-laminated windows are cracked to hell, but the rounds don't come all the way through.

THE LIMO slides broadly through a turn, sideslamming a parked van. Mace accelerates. Steckler's truck comes alongside, ramming them. The impact drives them sideways. Mace swerves to miss a light-standard and finds herself roaring between warehouse buildings which front the harbor.
The truck stays right with them.
Engelman fires bursts at the tires, shredding them off the rims.

The limo thunders along on steel rims, throwing rooster-tails of orange sparks.

Mace finds herself boxed-in by the buildings. No way to turn. Ahead is a short concrete pier. She hits the brakes and the limo skids on its rims out onto the pier, stopping before it reaches the end.
They are trapped.

Engelman and Steckler jump out of the truck, taking cover behind it. They rake the limo with bursts from their AK-47s. INSIDE THE CAR, it sounds like they are inside a steel drum in some psychotic Calypso band. But the armored body panels hold.
Lenny and Mace keep their heads down below the door-frame.
Lenny is calling 911 on his car phone.
He gets a no-service recording.
Mace has reloaded her Sig and is trying to open the door on her side (away from the bad guys). It is jammed, probably by the sideswiping.

Steckler reaches into the bed of the truck and pulls out a gallon gas can. He uncaps it and throws it across the pavement. It slides under the limo, glugging its contents onto the ground. Steckler grabs a road-flare from under the seat of the truck and strikes the cap, lighting it.
He tosses the flare under the limo—

KA-WHOOMPH!! The gas can explodes in a fireball. The Continental is engulfed in flames.
From the inside all Lenny and Mace can see is fire.
All the windows are covered in roaring flames.

This is bad, Mace says matter-of-factly. Lenny is freaking,

shouting that the gas tank will go any second. Mace isn't listening.
She's thinking.

She slams the car into gear and floors it.
The powerful Lincoln thunders forward. It crashes through a chain-link fence and launches right off the end of the pier.
A fireball plunging in a meteoric arc into the oily black water.
Inside, they are slammed forward by the impact.
The car sinks.
It hits bottom, twenty feet down.
It sits there amid old tires and junk. Shafts of light play down from the big streetlights at the end of the pier.
INSIDE, Lenny and Mace are in a flooding black tomb.

Are you out of your fucking mind? Lenny yells.

Fire's out, isn't it?

Mace scrambles into the backseat. She wrenches at the rear seatback—pulls it free.
She crawls half-into the huge trunk.
Water is up around their legs.
She grabs her shotgun . . . a sawed-off ten-gauge.

Mace looks over at Lenny. Tells him to get in there beside her. And to hold his breath.
She aims the ten-gauge at the trunk latch mechanism.

Lenny, kick out hard, then just follow me. Okay?

He nods. BLAM!! She blows the trunk latch into shrapnel.
The trunk lid belches open in a whoosh of bubbles.
Lenny and Mace kick out, heading toward the lights of the pier.

She gets alongside the slimy concrete wall and surfaces slowly.

Lenny comes up beside her.

They are in the inky shadows under a massive bumper made of rail-road ties. Engelman and Steckler are standing above them, scanning the water over the barrels of their AKs.

Let's get out of here, Steckler says.

What about the tape?

You going to go get it? Steckler shouts, pointing at the black water. They run back to the truck and high-tail out of there.

Down below, Lenny and Mace are clinging to the pier, chest deep in the water. They hear the truck pulling away.

They let out big exhalations of relief.

Lenny feels around in his jacket pocket. He pulls out the tape . . . nice and dry in its plastic case.

Holds it up to show Mace.

Are you impressed? he says.

CUT TO LENNY AND MACE, dripping wet, riding in the backseat of Curtis' car. They pull up at Mace's house and she thanks Curtis for picking them up. Cecile comes running out to meet them, asking if Mace is alright.

They go inside together. Zander is asleep.

Lenny goes straight to his playback gear and sets up the deck on the kitchen table.

Mace gets Zander up and tells Cecile to take him to her house, because she and Lenny are probably going out again.
Cecile says she and Curtis were going to a New Year's Eve party.
Mace says no. She doesn't want Cecile out on the streets tonight.
Curtis says *it's the party of the century, no way we sitting home.*
Mace gives him the look.
He puts up his hands. Okay. I'm with it.
We see that, at 27, Mace is the de facto matriarch of this family.
Cecile leaves the keys to her old Honda Civic and takes Zander, splitting with Curtis in his car.

Mace comes back in, going down the hall to the kitchen, where she finds Lenny, sitting at the table.
His eyes are closed as he plays back the tape Iris gave him.
As Mace sits down across from him, Lenny's mouth opens in shock.

Jesus, he whispers. He watches until the tape ends, then looks at her with a stunned expression.

Tell me, she says.

Lenny says she better see for herself.
Playback is against her religion, but Mace can tell by his expression it's no time to stand on principle.
She nods yes. He settles the trodes on her head.

I'm sorry this has to be your first wiretrip, he says. He hits PLAY.

Mace reacts as the sensory input hits her. She opens her eyes . . . realizes that she's seeing double. Lenny tells her to keep her eyes closed. She bites her lip as she lets the sensation of being another person flood through her.

POV SEQUENCE: We are Iris. Riding in a car. Fixing our makeup in a mirror on the passenger-side sunvisor. Iris flips the sunvisor back up, revealing the moving street. It is night.
We look down, and recognize the dress Iris was wearing when we first saw her, two nights ago. She puts her lipstick into a purse which is belted to her waist.
Iris turns her head and we see the driver.
It is JERIKO ONE.
He is laughing, talking to someone in the back seat.
Iris looks and we see REPLAY, Jeriko's sideman, and another woman, DIAMANDA. They are amorously entwined.

They are all laughing and passing around a bottle of Jim Beam. The car stereo is thumping loudly.
Iris' POV swings around and looks down, seeing Jeriko's

hand caressing her thigh. She puts her hand on his chest and leans close to him.
Jeriko grins, then looks up and swears.
We are aware of a wash of alternating red and blue light.

Shit. Fuckin' Five-O, Jeriko says.

Our POV swings to the rear-view mirror and we see an LAPD car behind us, with the gumball machine on. A spotlight hits us and we hear a single whoop on the siren. Jeriko pulls over, but they are on an overpass . . . no shoulder.

Go to the bottom of the ramp, comes a bullhorn voice from behind them. Jeriko and Replay are both swearing. He pulls the car down the ramp and they come to a stop on a deserted street in a warehouse district. Our POV looks around nervously.
Black shadows and concrete pillars. No one around. Cars whoosh on the bridge above but they might as well be on Mars.
The car is stopped next to a train yard. We hear the rumble of diesels nearby, the clank of freightcars.

We see the outlines of TWO COPS advancing through the beam of the spotlight, their guns drawn.

Jeriko can't believe this shit. He jumps out and the cops start yelling. Telling him to get down on his knees and put his hands on his head.
They are telling everyone to get out of the car.
Our POV comes up and out of the car.

Put your hands behind your head now, one of the cops is yelling at Jeriko, who is still giving them attitude.

They get Replay down on his knees as well, in the wet gutter next to the curb.

The cops are closer now.

We see that they are Steckler and Engelman.

Engelman turns to us and tells us to put our hands on the hood of the car and don't move. We exchange a look with Diamanda. Fucking cops.

Jeriko is winding up the cops. Not giving them the pleasure of the humiliation. You can see it escalating.

He says, *I suppose you stopped us cause you had suspects fitting our description in the area, what you're gonna tell me. What was the description? Two black guys in a car? Yeah, right, I heard that one before . . .*

Engelman pulls out Jeriko's wallet, looks at his ID.

Jeriko keeps going, *Well, you stopped the wrong guy tonight officer . . . what is it? Steckler. Officer Steckler. Cause I'm the 800-pound gorilla in your mist, fucker. I make more in a day than you make in a year, and my lawyers love to spend my money dragging sorry-ass Aryan robocops like you into court. Get a man down on the ground with no probable cause. Fuck you!* Steckler tells him to shut the fuck up and kicks him down on his face.

Diamanda starts yelling to leave them alone, they weren't doing anything.

Steckler says, *Shut up. Don't make me walk over there.*

Engelman shows the ID to Steckler, saying something we can't hear.

Steckler says to Jeriko, *You're Jeriko? That rap puke? Is that right? You're the one getting all the gangbangers to form citizens groups and go downtown . . . trying to rake the LAPD over a cheesegrater . . . all that shit?*

That's right. And you're gonna be in my next song, moth-erfucker, it's called Robo-Steckler. You gonna be famous.

Replay starts laughing. Diamanda stifles a giggle.
Steckler is white-lipped with rage. Years of frustration coming to a vibrating head of steam pressure. Too many disciplinary actions, too many suspensions, too little ap-preciation of the tough job they do.

Jeriko goes on, *It's a song about a cop who meets his worst nightmare, a nigger with enough political juice to crush his ass like a stinkbug.*

Steckler looks around the empty street. Looks at En-gelman.
Down at Jeriko, proned out on the pavement.

I don't think so, he says, and shoots him BLAM! BLAM!
Twice in the back of the head. Just like that.

Diamanda screams. Replay tries to roll to his feet.
Steckler shoots him twice in the stomach.
Replay is screaming. Rolling around holding his guts.

I don't hear you laughing! Steckler shouts at him.

Engelman is yelling something. Steckler turns to him.
His eyes are wide with adrenaline. Steckler orders him to get the bitches.
Engelman hesitates and then spins toward us.
Diamanda is screaming, backing away from Engelman.
Steckler shoots Replay four more times.
We spin 180 and start to run. Hear shots . . .
BLAM! BLAM! BLAM! Spin back . . . to see Diamanda dropping to her knees. Engelman shoots her again. Then raises his gun toward us.

We spin away. The world becomes a kinetic blur.

The sound of shots. We see puffs of dust on the ground in front of us. Missed shots. We tumble over a guardrail and roll down an embankment . . . get up and keep running.

Train tracks ahead. Looking back . . . here come Steckler and Engelman down the embankment, overtaking us.

We hear the thunder of a train . . . spinning again to look forward.

Freight train doing fifty on the nearest track. Almost to us.

We leap forward.

Over the track. The diesel roars past behind us.

Looking back . . . a black wall of moving steel.

Backing away from it.

We see Engelman and Steckler crouching down . . . trying to aim through the wheels. Hear the impotent pop of their guns over the roar of the train.

Turning to run again. We see a tiny hole appear in a sign right in front of us with a metallic SPANG.

Running and running.

Looking back.

No pursuit. Train still rolling by. Can't see the cops.

Running, running. Heart pounding and lungs heaving.

Sobbing sounds coming from somewhere, seeming to fill the night.

Looking down . . . one shoe on, one shoe off.

Iris's hand takes off the remaining shoe, clutches it to her chest.

We move forward into the dark train-yard as—
THE TAPE ENDS.

ON MACE, reacting. Stunned. She opens her eyes.
Lenny is on the phone nearby.
He says, *Hang on, Max.*

Lenny crosses and shuts off the playback deck, then hands her a drink. She gulps it. He picks up the phone again.

I'm back. So what the fuck do we do?

CUT TO MAX IN HIS CAR. He tells Lenny hell if he knows. But they can't talk cellular. Strictly landline. And he says don't trust anybody. *I mean nobody. Don't go to the cops . . . I'll tell you why when we get together. And don't get pulled over, for chrissake. Don't use any credit cards, they'll be scanning for your numbers. You'll pop up. You gotta be invisible. Listen, meet me at Tran's in half an hour.*

Yeah, okay. Gotta go, Max.

Mace is still reeling.
Even in the thick of it, chased by guys with machine guns, on fire driving off a pier, underwater . . . we never saw Mace scared.
She looks scared now.
This could be one they can't win.

No wonder Iris was so freaked, she says. *Poor thing. Do you know what this means, Lenny? If this gets out?*

Yeah. I got an idea.

If folks find out that the LAPD just flat-out executed Jeriko One? *My God.*

Lenny sticks his Glock in his waistband, over his right hip.

Look, we've gotta get out of here. Right now. These two whacko cops probably ran your plates while they were following us around. They'll have this address.

Mace gets it. She accepts what he says quickly. Matter-of-factly.
Yeah. Okay. Let me pack some stuff.

No. There's no time.

Lenny grabs his deck and trodes, pulling out the tape and putting it in his pocket. He heads down the hall to get his other stuff. He takes the box of Faith tapes and chucks them into his bag, along with the playback equipment.

Mace climbs up on the kitchen counter and pulls a black bag down from the top of the highest cabinet. She hops down and unzips it. Inside she has a .380 auto pistol and some ammo. She starts loading a magazine.

Lenny has his bag over his shoulder. He stops in the bathroom to take a leak for the road.

Mace clicks the magazine into the pistol and zips up the bag. She sets it on the kitchen table. She crosses to the fridge to pick up Cecile's car keys. Through the kitchen window she notices movement in the alley behind her house . . . a pickup truck with its lights off coming to a stop.

She hits the deck, shouting to Lenny, a microsecond before an AK-47 opens fire.

Lenny flops sideways into the tub, getting as low as he can. The drywall explodes inward as the assault rifle rakes the house.
Rounds hit the side of the tub, dimpling it from end to end.

The kitchen is torn to pieces by the bursts, which tear right through the walls like paper. Mace is showered with debris. Shattered glass. Flying plaster.

The water-cooler explodes. Mace, on her stomach, manages to get the fridge door open and hide behind it. The inner side of the door is riddled with hits, sending catchup, mustard and egg debris flying.

The room light is shot out, leaving only the fridge light.

Suddenly there is silence.

Mace, behind the fridge door, sees a shadow on the floor.
Someone is at the outside kitchen door.
She hears the splintered door open. Feet crunching on broken glass.
Her gun is on the table, across the room. She'd never make it.
Mace holds her breath. She reaches one hand silently up onto the top of the stove next to her head . . . searching.

In the light from the fridge, she sees something appear past the edge of the fridge door . . . a long fat silencer, screwed onto an Ingram MAC-10, held by gloved hands.

The man in the black ski mask sees her a split-second too late.
The iron skillet comes up under his hands, knocking the gun upward.
A burst goes into the ceiling. And Mace is on him.
She slams the intruder into the far wall, keeping her hands on the gun, trying to keep the muzzle away from her.
She cracks her forehead down on the bridge of his nose.
Knees him in the balls.
He *oophs* and folds over. She does it again.
She rips the gun out of his hands. It clatters away into the shadows. They struggle viciously in the dark, slipping and sliding on the flooded floor. The ski-mask gets pulled half-off, revealing Steckler the street-monster cop.

He snarls and rams her against the wall, outweighing her by
90 pounds. He pounds her head into the plaster.
Lenny comes in with his Glock.
Sees only dark shapes.

GIVE IT UP, STECKLER!

Steckler spins Mace around, between him and Lenny. He
gets her in a vicious headlock, using her body as a shield.
She can barely breathe.
Lenny pulls a hand out of his pocket . . . holding a squid
tape.

This is what you want. Take it and cut her loose.

Lenny moves warily forward . . . holding the tape far out
with one hand, holding the gun back with the other. Steckler
reaches out for the tape.
Takes it.
Then he suddenly hurls Mace at Lenny with incredible
force, knocking him down.
Mace hits the floor amid broken glass and water.
Steckler makes it out of the back door.
Mace scrambles to the MAC-10 and rolls to her knees into a
firing position.
But she ducks as—
Engelman opens fire again from the alley, raking the
kitchen.
Steckler makes it to the pickup and they floor it out of there.
Mace, pissed off beyond belief, runs right out the back door
after them.
She aims the MAC-10 at the pickup as it roars away.
Lenny comes out behind her.

Shoot! Lenny says.

Lenny, I got neighbors. I can't just go capping off toward Mrs. Dochard's house, for Chrissake!

I knew that.

I can't believe you gave him the tape.

Yeah, me neither. It was one of my favorites. Me and Faith in a hot tub on my birthday.

You didn't!

Yeah. I'm gonna really miss it. Come on, we gotta get outta here.

CUT TO THEM IN CECILE'S CIVIC. They see helicopters circling as they maneuver the dark streets. Xenon searchlights crisscross the rooftops nearby.
They see patrol cars passing on cross-streets, lights flashing. It feels like the entire LAPD is looking for them.
Same sense of fear/vast forces arrayed against you as with Iris running along the train tracks.

Mace says Steckler wanted the hit to look like a drive-by.
Very commonplace in her part of town. Nobody would question it.
So they hose us down from the alley, then creep in for a deal-closer with a silenced weapon . . . can't afford to leave anybody breathing.

Lenny is cranked up and paranoid.

Now he's got Gant's goons, a psycho sex-killer and the LAPD all trying to kill him. The new millenium is three hours away and it looks iffy he'll make it.
He doesn't know who they can trust.

They obviously can't go to the police.

Well, look at the plus side, Mace says, *You gave up your hot-tub tape to save me. That's real progress for you, Lenny.*

They approach a police checkpoint. Mace bluffs it through. Lenny slouches, shitting a brick the whole time as they go through.
As they drive, they see small crowds here and there, street parties in progress. People drinking and firing bottle rockets. Big police presence everywhere.

Mace says something is bothering her. She can't put the sophistication of Iris' killer with the brutal stupidity of those two cops. It doesn't add up.

Lenny says he doesn't think one of the cops killed Iris. He thinks that whoever Iris was wearing for was trying to break the trail back to them by killing her. *The thing that's driving me crazy is I know Faith is involved in this somehow. It's got to be her shitbird boyfriend. He's the only one that knows everybody. He was Jeriko's manager.*

Mace didn't know that. *Yeah,* Lenny says. *And he would know Iris through Faith. So that closes the loop. Jeriko plus Iris equals Philo Gant. But I still have no fucking idea what's going on here.*

THEY PULL UP in front of Tran's warehouse. There is no traffic on the street. Max is parked near the entrance, waiting. He flashes his headlights at them as they pull up to him. Max gets out of his car and joins them. They go in together.

Max says, *I pulled files on this guy Steckler. He's been suspended four times in eight years for excessive use of force. What they euphemistically refer to as a problem officer. His partner's name is Engelman. A hardcharger from gang task-force. Macho reputation. A real Nazi-youth. These guys pulling over Jeriko . . . you couldn't a planned a better train wreck.*

They buzz Tran's intercom. No answer. Lenny notices that the elevator cage is down, which is unusual. He raises one eyebrow and they step into it. Mace slips her .380 out, on alert.

The only sound is the clanking mechanism as they ascend. When they arrive at the floor there is no one in sight. They raise the safety bars and walk toward Tran's area.

Tran?
No answer.
They find him slumped in a chair, staring at nothing. Playback trodes are on his head. Somebody got to him.

Lenny examines him. He's seen this before. It's called a cook-off. You plug an amplifier into the output chip of the deck and it boosts the signal to a near-lethal level which fries the brain's sensory cortices. His lobes have been poached by sensory overload.
He is completely cut off from the outerworld.

Max says the psycho cops are on a slash and burn to track down any copies of the tape. Since Tran is a known duplicator, and totally plugged in to the wiretripping scene, it would be logical to interrogate him. Find out what he knows. Like: If copies were made. Or who might have wired up Iris. And afterward, this was a good way to shut him up. It doesn't even get investigated as a homicide, because he's still technically alive.

Lenny gets right in front of Tran's eyes.

He shouts at him, at the top of his lungs.

TRAN'S POV. We see a roaring blizzard of incohoate static. Somewhere in the middle of it is a suggestion of Lenny's face, almost invisible. We hear the tiniest ghost of his voice, like a radio playing two blocks away.

Vita comes in with two gangmembers, carrying fast-food bags.
She clocks the situation . . . Lenny crouched over the slumped Tran.
Vita whips out a little nickel-plated automatic and runs at Lenny, screaming. Lenny jumps back, palms up, talking fast.
It takes the combined efforts of Max, Mace and Lenny to talk her out of drilling him.
She pushes past him to Tran and pulls on him, yelling. Her jaded ultra-cool act vanishes. She breaks down sobbing.
She knows what has happened to him.
The effect is permanent.

Who did this? she wants to know.

Lenny shows her a bit of the Jeriko death clip. He says it was probably these guys. The faces of Steckler and Engelman are burned into her memory.
Max pulls Mace and Lenny aside.

                    MAX
     Listen, Lenny . . . there might be more to this than
     what you think, here.

                    LENNY
     Whaddya mean?

                    MAX
     All I'm saying . . . You don't know how high up the
     food chain this thing goes. I've heard stuff.

LENNY

What stuff?

MAX

Smoke. Rumors. I've heard stuff about a death squad.

MACE

What kind of death squad?

MAX

A *deadly* one. A Death Squad. A group a guys loyal to the ultra-hardline school. Guys that've had too many years of city hall and the commissions and the fucking media pissing down their necks, suspending cops right and left, tying their hands . . . while outta the other side a their mouths these same people're squealing, *Save us, save us, do something you fucking morons, crime is totally out of control.* Nobody knows shit about it, but there's something going on. These guys could be part of it.

LENNY

Christ.

MAX

Exactly. Get religion. So Lenny, I love you like my own blood, but don't walk near me in public, okay.

LENNY

Thanks, buddy.

MAX

I'm kidding.

LENNY

What about Internal Affairs?

MAX

I heard even some of them were in on this.

LENNY

Bullshit! Conspiracy paranoia.

MAX

The issue is not whether you are paranoid but whether you are paranoid *enough*. Don't forget, ultimately LAPD is a military organization. Push comes to shove, they take care of their own.

MACE

It seems like the only card we have to play is the tape. You know, get it to the media somehow.

LENNY

Yeah, blow it open.

MAX

Sure . . . they run that story on the six o'clock news, and by seven o'clock you got the biggest riot in history. They'll see the fuckin' smoke from Canada.

MACE

You saying we just pretend it didn't happen? It happened. It was a fucking execution.

MAX

Fine. Do you want blood running waist deep in the storm drains? You got two hundred thousand hungry jobless gangbangers who are gonna spread like a wave through this city and burn it to the ground. And the street cops ain't gonna be standing around this time either . . . when they see the fires start, its gonna be like a goddamn school bell. I guarantee they'll be capping off at anything that moves . . . it'll be all-out war and you know it. You want that on your head?

MACE

Look, let's just make a few copies of the damn tape and figure out what to do with it later.

Lenny pops the tape into Tran's master deck and sets up to make five copies.

LENNY

I'm going to get Faith. Is she still at Gant's?

MAX

Yeah. But that's not such a great idea—

LENNY

Where's Gant?

MAX

At the Mondo. But he's coming back to pick her up, they're going to the big mega-party later.

Lenny tells Max to go to the club and keep good eyeball on Gant. He takes three cellulars with scramblers from Tran's tech storage. One for each of them.

LENNY AND MACE pull up to the front gates of Gant's house in Cecile's beat up Civic. Lenny pushes the buzzer and Wade answers. Wade won't let him in, and won't let him talk to Faith. Recommends that he leave.

Lenny backs up the Civic and floors it at the gate, breaking the actuator arm. The wrought-iron gate swings inward with a crash and Lenny hears a burglar alarm go off. He pulls forward into the courtyard. He and Mace get out of the car. Floodlights come on.

Wade Beemer comes out, drawing a pistol, followed by two other security guys assigned to cover the house. Lenny and Mace are just standing there, unthreateningly. Faith comes running out of the front door, stopping Wade and the security team from getting violent.

Wade says he's calling the police. Faith yells, NO! Absolutely not. And then Lenny knows that she knows about the Jeriko tape.
It's what he thought. They can't afford to get cops involved. One of the security guys shuts down the hooting alarm. Everyone is tense, electrified.

Lenny says, *Well you ain't gonna have us arrested, so either shoot us or invite us in for a drink.* Faith tells them to come into the house.
Wade wants their guns.
Mace tells him no, she'll just keep hers, thanks.
Her eyes say try to take it, motherfucker.

Faith tells Wade and the others to back off, leave them alone.
Wade says he's calling Mr. Gant. *Fine,* she says.
We see Wade go to a phone.

They go into the living room. Lenny has obviously never
been here. He looks around. Comments on the place.
She has done well for herself. Of course, at what cost?
Faith says he was unbelievably stupid to come here. Philo's
guys have standing orders to hurt him.

Mace gets right to the point. *What was Iris doing riding
around with Jeriko, wearing a wire?*
Faith says she doesn't know what Mace is talking about.

Lenny grabs her shoulders and shakes her. He says that
somebody took Iris, raped her then put a piece of cord
around her neck and twisted it until she stopped moving.
She turns away from them and starts to cry.
Mace says, *Look, the man just don't want to see you wind
up like that. Now talk to him, cause we don't have much
time.*

Faith asks if she can talk to Lenny alone.
Lenny, surprisingly, says no. Mace is in this.
She needs to hear whatever Faith has to say.
Faith nods.
Philo's become obsessed with playback, she says, *a total
wiretrip junkie. Always having me do clips for him, buying
new equipment. And he was getting more and more into
surveillance. Having people followed and videotaped. He
did this kind of shit all the time. You wouldn't believe some
of the stuff he would do. Recording the calls his business
partners made. Wiring up people left and right. He was
completely losing it. I mean, look at this house . . . there.
And there.*
She points at the cameras, watching every room.

*So then this beef with Jeriko came up. There was a big rift
between them. They were fighting over content on the new
album. Philo was afraid Jeriko was going to dump him and
get a new label, and a new manager. But he wasn't sure
about it, so he started with the surveillance. A couple nights
ago he wires up Iris and sends her and the other girl, Diamanda, over to Jeriko's table with his compliments.*

That night Iris calls up, freaking.

*I go pick her up. Philo watches the tape and just loses it. He
backhands her across the room.*

He can't believe the disaster she's gotten him into.

Suddenly it's all about him. Selfish prick.

So he gives her some cash.

*Tells her to check into the hotel under a wrong name and
wait till he figures out what to do. He's terrified the cops will
find her, and beat it out of her who she was working for, and
come looking for him. And since I know about it, he says
I'm in danger too.*

(we could see some of this in flash-cut flashback form—just
to break the monologue)

                          MACE

Do you have any recordings made by Gant?

                          FAITH

No. He never wears, only plays back. For him it's
about seeing himself through other people's eyes.
He's fascinated by his own image. Why do you
want to know?

                          MACE

Iris' killer has some kind of visual distortion.

                          FAITH

You think Philo killed her?

LENNY

Who knows about the cops killing Jeriko, besides
you and Gant?

FAITH

Joey Corto.

LENNY

Then it's either Gant himself or he had Corto do it.

FAITH

I can't believe it. What a nightmare.

Faith goes out to the pool. Lenny follows, motioning Mace
to stay back. He puts his hands on her shoulders.
Faith accuses Lenny of getting Gant into this stuff in the
first place. And he got her into it, too. It's like an obsession,
and it's all his fault.

LENNY

I guess I thought if I got you to wear the trodes, if
you could just see yourself the way I did, through
my eyes . . . you would know how much you were
loved. But watching and seeing are two different
things.

FAITH

I always loved your eyes, Lenny. *(she touches his
eyelids)* I loved the way they saw.

LENNY

Will you leave here with me, right now.

FAITH

Yes, Lenny. Thank you. My guardian angel.

She kisses him. It is soulful, not erotic.

INSIDE THE HOUSE, Mace watches them kiss in the shimmering light from the pool. She turns away.
The cellular in her pocket rings.
It is Max who says that Philo and his goons had already left the club by the time he got there. So he figures they could be almost back to the house by now. Mace clicks off and goes out to interrupt Lenny and Faith. *We're out of here,* she says.

Lenny tells Faith they have to go right now.
She wants to grab some things.
Mace says, *Uh unh, now.*

They are going down the front steps when Wade intercepts them.
Faith says she's going out, she'll be back in a few minutes.
Wade says Mr. Gant gave him orders that she was not to leave.

At that moment a STRETCH LIMO pulls into the courtyard at high speed. Philo and Joey Corto get out of the back while Constance and Duncan come out the front doors. The men are in tuxes, Constance in an elegant white gown.

Mace says, *Lenny, don't try anything. Just keep your hands in plain sight.*

Everybody is tense, moving slowly. Everybody knows everybody has a gun. An armed society is a polite society.
Philo walks up to Lenny. They eyeball each other.
Gant turns to Faith, saying, *I thought we had a party to go to, my dear.*
The party of the century. You're not standing me up, are you?

Forget it, Philo. I'm leaving with Lenny.

No, I don't think so. We have to at least put in an appear-ance, tonight. What would people think? Now why don't you go in and get ready. You can wear those pearls I gave you. Say goodbye to Lenny.

The implication is that Philo is going to have his team do bad things to Lenny if she doesn't play ball.

Faith goes up to Philo. Gets very close. She says, *You want me at the party, at your side, smiling for the cameras . . . you want me to play ball with you and keep my mouth shut? Then you let Lenny drive out of here. Right now, Philo. Do it. Don't fuck with me.*

Without warning Philo rabbit-punches her right in the gut.
She gasps and drops to one knee.
Lenny lunges forward and Mace grabs him.
All the bodyguards whip their guns out. Lenny and Mace are staring down six large-caliber muzzles.
Mace keeps her hands in view, empty.

Whoah, whoah, she says, *everybody just stay chill.*

She stands between Lenny and Philo, pushing back on Len-ny's chest with one hand. Constance and Corto in particular look like they would love to start cranking off rounds.

Don't play his game, Mace says low to Lenny.

Philo's eyes glitter. He looks from her to Lenny, to Mace, back to Faith. He seems unspeakably evil, somehow, but so icily under control that it's scary. He is mentally reviewing his options . . . one of which is to kill Lenny immediately.

PHILO

Everybody just take it down a notch. This is no
way to end a millenium. Tonight we should be cele-
brating.

Lenny looks at Philo, wondering what his game is. If he is
the killer, then he has been sending Lenny the tapes for a
reason, goading him to do something. But what?

PHILO

There's no need for you to hang around, Lenny.

MACE

Get in the car. Right now.

LENNY

I'm not leaving without Faith.

FAITH

Get out of here, Lenny. I don't need your help.
You're just making it worse. Can't you see that? Go
on!! Get out of my life! Just leave me alone.

Faith is going it to save him, but she is convincing.
Mace pushes Lenny into the Honda Civic.
Gets in herself and starts backing away.

THEY RUN INTO MAX, COMING UP THE HILL, pull
over and talk. (or car phone)

Lenny says, *I'm pretty sure Gant's the killer. It's either
Gant or Corto.*

Naw. Corto's too stupid. It's Gant. Where's Faith?

We gotta go back for her.

*Look, don't panic. He's not gonna do her at his own house
and draw all that attention. He'll do her at the party.
He took a suite at the Bonaventure, right in the middle of
the action. So after the glitzy shindig down in the ballroom,
he takes her upstairs for a little champagne . . . that's when
he makes his move.*

*Okay, Max, you stay here and follow them when they leave.
Whatever you do, keep them in sight.*
(to Mace)
Come on. We're going to a party.

MACE IS DRIVING in silence. They hear sirens across the
night. Two large pillars of fire are visible several blocks
away.
There are dark crowds of people everywhere.
People on the sidewalks, lighting fireworks. There are
flashes and explosions. It could be a celebration, or a war-
zone. Maybe both. Or one about to turn into the other.

Lenny tenses up as they go through a police checkpoint near
their destination, Cecile's apartment. Mace says, *They never
stop you going in, they don't give a shit about you going in.*

LENNY AND MACE pull up to Cecile's apartment. It is
only two miles southeast of the Bonaventure in downtown
LA but it might as well be another planet. It is gang terri-
tory pure and simple. Blacks and Hispanics. Graffiti everywhere. Burned-out buildings.
The pull up to Cecile's. It is a really poor neighborhood.
Lenny has probably never been to a place like this. He sees
abject poverty, here.
Even so, people are partying.
There are some homeboys chillin' on the front steps who
give Mace the local hand-sign. She returns it automatically
as she goes up the steps past them. An ex-homegirl. Lenny

gets out of the car with his wardrobe bag. The homeboys give Lenny the eye as he brushes past them. Mace says, *He's with me.*
Curtis and Cecile are on the balcony of her apartment, lighting off bottle rockets. Zander is still up, because of all the excitement, even though he's not supposed to be.
Mace says he can stay up and watch the fireworks.

Mace and Lenny go inside. They both look like shit and if they're going to crash a ritzy party, they need to change.
He opens his bag and pulls out the suit he packed.
He glances at her. She's just standing there with her jaw locked.

> **LENNY**
> Come on. We don't have much time.

> **MACE**
> I'm not going.

> **LENNY**
> What?

> **MACE**
> It's a set-up, Lenny. You're gonna run down there to save your fair lady, and you're gonna wind up dead on the floor next to her. That's why they been sending you those tapes, to get you crazy. So you'll rush in, without thinking.

> **LENNY**
> I'm going.

He turns away, starting to get changed.
Mace's anger is out of frustrated concern for him.

She grabs his shoebox full of Faith tapes. Holds them up to him.

MACE
You are a pussywhipped sorry-ass motherfucker, you know that? You gonna get yourself killed for this . . . this toxic-waste bitch.

She dumps the box of tapes on the floor. She starts stomping on them with one heel, crunching several into junk. Lenny freaks out and scrambles to pick them up, trying to stop her, push her away.
They struggle for a pathetic, tragic moment.
Mace snaps. She grabs him by the lapels and swings him around, slamming him back against a wall.

MACE
Lenny! This is your life, Lenny! Right here. Right now. This is real-time. Not playback. Real-time. Time to get real. Understand what I'm saying . . . she doesn't love you. Maybe she did once, I don't know, but she doesn't now. These are used emotions. It's time to trade them in.

Mace's tone becomes more gentle. We see that her outburst is, beneath it all, coming from a place of compassion.

MACE
Lenny, memories were meant to fade. They're designed that way for a reason.

Lenny seems to crumple. He knows he has to let go. But it is so painful.

LENNY
Have you ever been in love with somebody who didn't return that love?

Mace gives him a look like, jeez Lenny, are you dumb sometimes.

MACE

Yeah, Lenny. I have.

LENNY

It didn't stop you from loving them. Right? Or understanding them, or being able to forgive them . .

MACE

I guess.

LENNY

And it didn't stop you from wanting to protect
them. Did it?

MACE

No. It didn't.

Lenny's eyes are brimming with tears. He makes no attempt
to hide it . . . doesn't brush them away.

LENNY

When I was working Vice I saw every fucking de-
pravity known to the human animal. This city was
one big toilet to me . . . I was lost, Mace. I was in
outer darkness. Right before I left the force . . .
got thrown out . . . I busted this scrawny strung-
out little teeny-hooker. She was just another runaway giving twenty dollar blowjobs to buy crank.
You know, another lost soul. Her name was Faith.
She had these shoes with broken straps, and her
knees were knocking together.

MACE

You never told me about this, Lenny.

LENNY

She was different . . . different from the other suck-zombies wandering up and down the boulevard. There was a light in her eyes that I'd never seen before. And she had this *voice*. It was scary, all that pain coming out of that little body. Like she could take all the hurt and rage of the entire world and lift it up to heaven in one voice. I promised her I'd help her. That I'd always be there to protect her. (long pause) So . . . see? It doesn't much matter whether she loves me. I still have to go.

Mace takes his face in her hands. She kisses him lightly on the cheek, where the tear-track is.
Then she nods, consigning them to their destinies.

MACE

Okay, Lenny. Let's get ready.

CUT TO FIFTEEN MINUTES LATER.

ON LENNY, adjusting the knot of his tie. He has put on the suit he's been lugging around. Mace comes out of Cecile's bedroom and Cecile whistles approvingly.

CECILE

That dress fit you girl. I'm never gonna see it again, now.

MACE

It's a little tight.

Mace is wearing a short black cocktail dress, very sheer. It's cut low at the top and high at the bottom, showing plenty of her muscular legs. The high heels are doing good things for her calves.

Mace's braided hair is loose and full, around her shoulders, like the mane of a lion. She is even wearing lipstick and eye-makeup.

She looks hot.

Mace unselfconsciously hikes up the dress and adjusts the Velcro on the elastic-holster strapped to her right thigh.

She is all business as she slips her .380 auto into the holster and pulls the dress down. You can't see the gun, hidden between her upper thighs, just above the hemline. In fact, it looks like she couldn't be concealing a quarter anywhere on her body.

Lenny glances at Mace and does a double take.

She is a girl. He is caught by a sudden realization of her woman-ness. He sort of freezes for a second, appraising her. She scowls at him.

                                MACE
        Come on, let's roll.

He slips the Glock into his waistband behind his right hip and hurries to catch up with her as she goes out the door.

IT IS THE MOTHER OF ALL PARTIES. There must be 100,000 people in the closed streets around the Bonaventure. Arc lights sweep the sky. There are two outdoor bandstands, with live music pounding. There are lasers, strobe-lights. People are literally dancing in the streets.

Huge projection video screens are set up all over the place. It looks like a U-2 concert ten blocks long. The idea is to tie into a global event. LA is connected to other cities all over the world by satellite, sharing in the celebration in different time zones.

The excitement has been building all evening as midnight sweeps across the country toward the West Coast.

It is a multimedia extravaganza.

Lenny and Mace are stuck in stopped traffic a couple of blocks away.

He is looking at his watch and cursing. People are streaming all around the cars. They hear the loud thump of music over a PA. People pound on the Civic as they go by, or press their faces against the glass. A fight breaks out between some drunken grunge-rockers, and people scramble over the hood of the car to get out of the way. Cops run in, chasing the combatants off into the swirling mass of humanity.

Lenny and Mace bail out of the car, abandoning it in the middle of the madness. They head into the crowd on foot.

Mace leads the way, pushing through the crowd toward the hotel. We see her bodyguard training in the way she positively moves people out of the way.

They will move through the various strata of society as they

work their way in to the party's inner sanctum in the huge
tent which has been set up as a kind of ballroom adjacent to
the hotel.

The street crowd is jeans and T-shirts. No admission. Beer
and hotdogs. This of course is the vast majority of the crowd,
and we see all types, from yuppie couples to black and Lat-
ino gangbangers cruising in posses. We catch a glimpse of
Vita Minh and Tran's Vietnamese gang pushing through the
crowd.

Further in is a more exclusive section. You pay to get in.
There are tables and a huge buffet. Champagne in plastic
glasses.

A dance floor. Recorded music . . . an assortment of hits from
various decades, from swing through fifties, to top 40 of the
seventies, eighties, and nineties. This is an upscale crowd,
but not the creme.

At the center is the glitterati event . . . the LA New Year's
Ball. Red carpets and papparazzi, movie stars and politicians. Lots of tuxes and gowns, diamonds sparking back the
spotlights of the video crews.

It is like all of LA, from poorest to richest, compressed down
into a few square blocks.

There are cops everywhere. Cops on motorcycles, cops in
cars, cops in riot gear. One of the uniforms turns.

It is Steckler. He says something into his rover. Scanning
the crowd.

Steckler doesn't see Mace and Lenny pass 50 feet behind
him as they approach the entrance to the ball. But Mace
spots him, and points him out to Lenny. Oh shit. They turn
away when he glances their direction.

Lenny pulls out his flip-phone and calls Max, jamming a finger in his ear to block out the din.

INSIDE THE BALL we see Max, wearing an ill-fitting tux. The glitterati crowd is elbow to elbow. He answers the phone ringing in his pocket.
Yeah? Lenny, where the hell are you, pal?
Max gives him a situation report. He has positive eyeball on Faith and Gant. OFF MAX'S LOOK TO:

GANT'S TABLE, where Philo and Faith are sitting with music and entertainment biz types. The crowd in here is all about power, money, and glitz. Faith gulps her champagne. She looks cold, uninterested. She is wearing a low-cut maroon gown, matching lipstick. With her black hair and pale skin she looks like an elegant vampire. There is a string of pearls around her throat.
Corto, Constance, Wade and Duncan are circulating nearby. Max hangs up and shifts position so he can see Faith clearly.

CU FAITH, turning toward Max. Her eyes connect with his through the passing partiers. She gives him a strange little smile.
As if to say, I know you're watching me.

She turns to Gant, pulling him out of some animated record business conversation, and tells him she can't stand the charade any longer. She's going up to the suite to get drunk.

GANT

Fine. I'll be up in fifteen minutes, so we can have a little New Year's toast.

FAITH

Take your time.

GANT

Constance will walk you up.

FAITH
Whatever.

Constance stays right next to Faith as she leaves.
Gant finds Max with his eyes.
He points with one finger. As if to say *you go too.*
Max nods and saunters after Faith and Constance.

OUTSIDE, Lenny and Mace slip into lines with the flow of
people getting out of their limos, heading into the ball.
Lenny deftly swipes somebody's invitation as he and Mace
push past them in the line.
He reads it. 500 bucks a plate. Unbelievable.
They get past the ushers checking tickets.
Then they smoothly slip past the guys with metal detectors,
who are buried with the volume of people.

Lenny scans the ballroom as they walk in. The place is huge.
It takes them a while to locate Gant's table. No Faith. Lenny
calls Max.

CUT TO MAX in the red-carpeted foyer of the hotel. His
voice is low as he follows Faith some distance back. He tells
Lenny that he has Faith in sight. She's going up to the suite.

What's the suite number?

*1267. But I need you to get in there and keep an eye on
Gant and his crew. I'll get to Faith and bring her down the
firestairs. Call you back.*

Lenny and Mace are skirting the dance floor, keeping Gant
in sight across the room. Lenny sees Corto coming toward
them.
Corto hasn't spotted them yet, so Lenny takes Mace in his

arms and dances with her, sort of hiding his head in her
mane as Corto passes.

Lenny is suddenly intensely aware of Mace's body pressed
against his. He separates from her and they both awkwardly
step back.

Lenny points to a man sitting at a table with a bunch of city
hall types. He is in his late fifties, stern and flinty eyed, with
military short hair. Even in a tux he looks like a Marine
Corps general. Or maybe a Calvinist minister.

LENNY

See that guy. The one with the ramrod up his ass?

MACE

Yeah. You know him?

LENNY

That's Deputy Commissioner Palmer Strickland.
He used to be the head of Internal Affairs. He's
the guy that had me thrown off the force.

MACE

What are you thinking?

LENNY

I'm going to give him the tape. I know this prick
. . . his ass is so tight when he farts he makes a
sound only dogs can hear. If there is a conspiracy,
this is the one cop that I know ain't in it.

MACE

What if you're wrong?

LENNY

Then we'll be right where we are right now.

                              MACE
Fucked.

                              LENNY
That's right. Hang here, I'm going to make a move.

Strickland excuses himself and leaves his table.
Lenny glances back at Mace, not wanting to separate too
far, then decides to follow Strickland. Mace watches him disappear into the crowd, then turns to scan the room, not lik-
ing the way it's going.

WADE BEEMER spots Mace through the dancers and goes
to Joey Corto. Corto scowls and they start toward her. We
see Corto on a walkie to Duncan, who is elsewhere in the
room.
Mace turns and starts away through the swarming partiers.
Corto signals to Wade to separate and try to flank her in a
pincer movement. The three of them moving with purpose
through the oblivious crowd.

Palmer Strickland goes into the men's room. Lenny follows
him.
The men's room is a cavernous affair. A few guys in tuxes
wandering around, pissing and checking their hair.
Strickland goes to a urinal. Lenny goes to one that's two
over from him.

                              LENNY
Hello, Deputy Commissioner.

                            STRICKLAND
Hello. Do I—? Oh, Nero. How appropriate that I
should be talking to *you* in a toilet.

Lenny opens his coat and pulls out . . . his playback deck.
The one he sometimes clips to his belt like a walkman.
He reaches over and puts it on the top of Strickland's urinal.

LENNY

There's a tape in there you need to see. I mean
right now.

While Lenny is looking at Strickland, a young LAPD OFFI-
CER comes out of a stall, and goes to the sink. He glances
in the mirror at Lenny.

STRICKLAND

This is illegal equipment. With your record, you
could do hard time for this.

LENNY

Same self-righteous prick I remember. Look, this
ain't a setup, there's no tricks, here. I'm clean.
See—

Lenny tugs painfully hard on his own hair, opens his jacket,
pulls up his shirt to show his bare chest . . . a strange dance
indicating he is not wired. From Strickland's perspective he
seems like a loon . . . edgy and paranoid. Totally unstable.

LENNY

No wire. No tricks. Just look at the tape, Strickland. Come on, you like surveillance, you've seen
plenty of these things. Just go in the stall right
now and hit PLAY.

The young cop steps up behind Lenny.

YOUNG COP

(to Strickland) Sir, is there a problem here?

Lenny turns. Oh shit. He edges toward the door. The cop is
looking at Strickland like . . . do I grab him?

STRICKLAND

Nero, maybe you better stick around for a while
until I can look into this more fully.

LENNY

I'll pass.

The cop takes his arm. Lenny twists viciously out of the grip,
pushing the cop away from him, and lunges for the door.
He makes it through and sprints into the crowd, with the
young cop charging after him.

STRICKLAND picks up the deck and scowls at it. His expression is opaque.

ON LENNY, sprinting through the busy kitchen, where
scores of cooks and servers are bustling around, cleaning up
from dinner.
He ducks into a huge walk-in cooler. He's ditched the cop, so
he pulls out his flip-phone, punching up Mace's number.

MACE answers in the ballroom crowd. He tells her he
thinks he may have screwed up bad. Before she can answer,
Mace is grabbed from behind by DUNCAN. He gets her in
a good tight come-along. Like any good security person, the
hold is not so obvious that the party around them is dis-
rupted.

LENNY now can't get an answer from Mace. He thinks the
call broke up, so he dials again.

CUT TO Mace's phone ringing, lying on the ballroom floor.

MACE IS WALKED around behind the bandstand. Corto
and Wade meet them there. Joey Corto walks up to her,

looking mean and smug. The stitches on his nose and the bruised swelling are a reminder of his last run in with her.

Mace twists one hand free and snaps it out in a blur. Her open palm breaks Corto's nose with an audible crunch. Corto screams and grabs his face, reeling back.

> **CORTO**
> Aw, not the fucking nose!!

She slams her foot down on Duncan's instep and snaps her head back simultaneously in a reverse head-butt. He manages to keep the hold, so Mace drives her free hand back into the approximate position of his nuts. Even though Duncan looks like he bench-presses Buicks, this has the desired effect. Mace jerks away from him, shoving him back through a buffet table, just as Wade moves in. Suddenly she's standing there with her dress hiked up and her pistol straight-armed, with the muzzle right in his face.

Wade backs up.

> **WADE**
> Hey, enjoy the party.

Mace spins and sprints through dumfounded glitterati, her gun innocuously tight to her side.
She makes it to one wall of the ballroom tent, and dives under.

OUTSIDE she finds herself amongst the street crowd, who don't even notice her. She holsters the gun and moves away from possible pursuit.

LENNY works his way back into the ballroom. Sees Gant is gone from the table. He's completely lost track of him. And there's no sign of Mace. He tries to call Max. No answer. Tries again. Starting to panic. Nothing. Fuck.

CUT TO LENNY in the hotel elevator. He is hyperventilating.

It's all going wrong. The doors open on the twelfth floor. He walks out. Standing at the corner, where she can watch the elevators and the corridor, is Constance.

Lenny doesn't break stride. Just walks toward her. He's tipped over. He's not afraid anymore. He's pissed off. She moves toward him.

LENNY
Constance, I don't want any trouble here.

We think he's starting the usual negotiation. But when he gets in range he lets fly with a line-drive right, straight into Constance's face. We're talking a John Wayne haymaker punch.

She staggers back, surprised and dazed, and he knees her right in the gut as hard as he can. Payback's a bitch, Constance.

She drops to her knees, winded. He draws his Glock and puts it behind her ear, pulling a pair of handcuffs off his belt. Okay, we're starting to believe he might have been a cop once.

CUT TO THE STAIRWELL. Lenny finishes handcuffing Constance to the stair railing.

CUT TO MACE, moving through the insane crowd. She is trying to work her way around to a service entrance back into the hotel.

The sky explodes with purple light as huge fireworks go off overhead. A crack like thunder follows. Then more flashes. The countdown to midnight has begun.

The party is building to a crescendo. It seems to have a sur-real, nightmarish quality. She passes a mime in a clock suit, who keeps adjusting the hands closer to midnight.

Mace is scanning warily as she moves. She turns and sees Engelman in the crowd, not twenty feet from her. He is look-ing right at her. Not recognizing her for a moment. Then . . . he realizes who she is.
He goes for his gun and Mace pushes people out of the way, breaking into a run. Engelman charges after her, pulling out his rover to call Steckler.

LENNY MOVES DOWN THE CORRIDOR to the suite at the end. He reaches the door. 1267. Sees that the door is ajar. Always a bad sign. Lenny apprehensively enters the suit, with his gun two-handed in the low-ready position. His heart is pounding.
It is a luxurious corner suite with big balconies and an in-credible view of the high-rise district. The lights are out, and the rooms are silent.

Lenny can barely breathe from the tension as he moves through the living room. He notices that one balcony door is open. The roar of the crowd comes in like the sound of surf from far below. Fireworks explode across the sky, and the cheers from below sound like screams.

His feet crunch on broken glass . . . a shattered champagne bottle.
A lamp is knocked over. He reaches the door to the bedroom and looks in. The room is empty. The bed is unmade, the bedspread and sheet pulled off. One whole wall of the bed-room is mirrored.
Lenny looks back at the living room.
Suddenly he notices something on the coffee table.
It is an envelope, with NERO hand-printed on it.

He is drawn to it, hypnotically.
He opens it . . . and a squid-tape falls out into his hand.
This is like some kind of surreal dream.

STECKLER AND ENGELMAN are stalking Mace through the crowd. Steckler catches a glimpse of her running and he charges after her, like a bull, with his gun drawn. He hammers through anybody that gets in his way. Mace, sprinting through the crowd, sees an apparition ahead of her . . . a guy wearing Death's Head make-up and a black shroud, carrying a huge cardboard scythe in one hand and a doll (New Year's Baby) in the other. Death watches her pass.

LENNY, moving like he is in a trance, puts the trodes on his head.
TIGHT ON THE PLAY BUTTON as his finger punches down.

IN POV we approach room 1267. It is the familiar monochromatic vision of the killer. Our hands open the door quietly with a key-card. We enter the suite.
Some of the lights are on.
We see Faith out on the balcony. Watching the sea of madness below. She comes back in, carrying an empty champagne glass. She grabs a bottle off an end-table and up-ends it. Empty. She hurls it across the room, and it shatters against the wall.
Faith grabs the pearl necklace and rips it away from her throat in a paroxysm of rage and self-loathing.

We approach her, standing with her back to us, in her misery. Closer. Only a few feet now. She whips around, startled. Gasping loudly.
But then . . . she recognizes the wearer.
Oh, I didn't hear you come in, she says.
THE RECORDING STOPS, in a blast of static.

Lenny jerks at the discontinuity in the input, he is so keyed up.

THE RECORDING RESTARTS:
A new image resolves out of static.
Faith is pushed roughly down on the bed. We climb onto the bed, straddling her, and she gasps. We turn her onto her back.
She has been blindfolded.
The Wearer goes SSSHHH. A warning. Like the hiss of a snake.
Our hands seize her wrists and handcuff them one by one to the iron frame at the head of the bed.
The hands go out of sight and then reappear holding a set of trodes.
They are placed on her head . . . the spidery gecko-hand device almost disappearing in her black hair.

LENNY's guts have turned to water. He is shaking his head in horror, going No, no, no . . .

IN POV we see one of our hands come up holding the yellow plastic razor knife. The blade clicks out to its full length.
Our hands reach down and slowly slit her dress open, starting between her breasts and going down out of sight. She groans, squirming away from the cold knife.
The killer's hands open the material, exposing her white body, which in his peculiar vision is pure ivory. The knife deftly cuts off her panties.
We unbuckle our pants and reach for her, grasping her hips, pulling her to us.

ON LENNY, gagging. Overcome by revulsion and horror, mixing obscenely with the pleasure flooding into him from the tape.

**BACK TO POV as we pull our belt out of the beltloops
of our pants and wrap it around Faith's neck. Faith begins to pant in tiny rapid breaths. We tighten the belt
slowly.**

LENNY tears the trodes from his head. He clutches his
stomach, gasping for breath. Carrying the playback deck, he
staggers into the bedroom . . . to the bed. He stares wildly
around the room.
Beyond the bed he spots a shape.
It is covered in the bedsheet, but it is clearly a human form,
propped up against the wall on the far side of the nightstand.
He missed it in his earlier look from the bedroom door.

Lenny moves around the bed and reaches down to the foot
of the figure, grasping the edge of the sheet with a trembling
hand.
With horrified apprehension he pulls on the sheet.
It reveals the head and upper body of . . .
Philo Gant.

The last thing he expected. Lenny leans close and sees that
Gant is breathing shallowly, but his eyes are vacant. He
looks like Tran did. Lenny sits on the bed and puts the
trodes back on.
The fireworks and screaming outside sound like some night-
marish war, like the sound of the world coming to an end.
But all Lenny cares about is what's on the tape.
He hits PLAY.

**THE POV CONTINUES where it left off. Faith's body
lurches with the Wearer's thrusts. His hand tightens the
belt.**
Lenny feels the climax building.
Faith's body shakes as the killer comes . . . she cries out

herself, in pain . . . or is it? The killer's hand releases the belt. We see Faith gasping for breath and moaning.

Suddenly the POV whips sideways to the mirrored closet doors along one wall. In the mirror is a reflection of the bed and on it Faith. And on her . . . Max.

Still wearing his tux shirt, his pants down, her legs pulled up around him. They are both gasping for breath, spent, following their shattering orgasms. He runs his hands over her sweat-slick belly.

LENNY is stunned beyond his power to imagine.
He does not have the strength or the will to stop the tape.

IN POV we see Max's hands remove her blindfold. She looks right at us, still gasping with the aftershocks of her pleasure.

Max's hands undo the handcuffs, freeing her. She reaches for us, her eyes glittering with sated lust.

We slump forward onto her, and her face fills the POV.

FAITH

I love you.

Lenny is reeling with these revelations. His best friend is the killer. And the woman he loved loves him.

But the tape is not over . . .

THE POV CONTINUES as Max's eyes whip around in response to a sound behind them. The bedroom door is opening. Philo Gant is standing there with a shocked expression.

Like lightning we are off the bed, snatching our .45 from the nightstand and whipping around . . . putting the muzzle right in Gant's face. We pull him roughly across the room, too stunned to resist.

He is cursing Faith, cursing us.
We slam him back against the mirror wall and jam the
muzzle of the gun right in his mouth . . . a deadly gag.
Using the gun we push him down until he is sitting on
the floor with his back to the mirror.

Our eyes whip to Faith. She is freaking. Our eyes snap
back and forth between Philo and her. We see Max's reflection in the mirror as he talks to her, talking fast.

> **MAX**
> This piece a puke hired me to kill you, baby. Do
> you believe that? Isn't that right, Philo? You
> pinhead.

> **FAITH**
> Why?

> **MAX**
> Why do you think? You were starting to jam
> him with this Jeriko thing. He knew it was
> going to cost him for you to keep your mouth
> shut, and keep costing, so . . .

> **FAITH**
> But he was going to drop my recording deal,
> and pull the video, and kick me out with noth-
> ing. I had to do something!

> **MAX**
> No question. Bring me the trodes, baby. Come
> on, quick.

> **FAITH**
> What're you going to do?

Max doesn't answer. He puts the trodes on Philo's head and pulls something out of his pocket. It is a booster box. He plugs it into the deck. He takes the gain control and cranks it all the way up. He's setting up a cook-off. Gant's eyes go wide when he figures that out.

FAITH
You can't just kill him.

MAX
Yeah? Well, he was going to kill you. And this ratfuck paid to have Iris killed, to save his own sorry ass.

Gant tries to protest at that point but Max jams the gun deep into his throat, up to the trigger guard, choking off his words.

MAX
<u>You shut the fuck up, right now, I'm gonna pull this fuckin trigger!</u>

<u>K-BANG!!</u>
Faith shrieks, thinking Max shot him. But it's just the start of the fireworks outside (remember all this has already happened relative to Lenny entering the suite).

MAX
He's totally paranoid. No telling what he might do. Too much watching will do that to you. Look, baby, I don't see any choice here. It's now or never, the guy is a known input junkie, so a little OD won't surprise anybody. And it ain't murder anyway. He'll still be alive.

FAITH
My God.

We don't know if her reaction is to the horror of what is about to happen, or to the realization that she has the capacity to let it happen.

MAX

I love you, baby, you know I do, and it's the only way we can be together.

She stares, transfixed, as Max reaches for the deck.
He punches PLAY. She doesn't try to stop him.
Max puts his hand over Philo's mouth to muffle his screams as the input hits his brain like a screaming chainsaw of static from Hell.
The screaming outside, the pandemonium, give the moment a special madness.

The POV turns, looking out the window . . . staring fixedly at burst after burst of brilliant fireworks. Like the fireworks inside Gant's head.
THE TAPE ENDS.

Lenny takes off the trodes. He is wrung out, drenched with sweat.
We see that there is a figure standing in the doorway behind him.
Lenny turns, not surprised to see Max there with his .45 aimed at Lenny's chest. Max's surgical gloves look incongruous with his tux.

MAX

Don't make any assumptions about our friendship, Lenny.

LENNY

No. I suppose not. Given the historical perspective.

Max moves up to him cautiously, and takes the Glock out of Lenny's waistband. Lenny stands up, slowly.

MAX

I'll have that. Glock 23. Nice.

LENNY

Where's Faith?

MAX

I sent her back down to the party. I figured I'd wait up here until you killed Gant.

LENNY

What makes you think I'm gonna kill Gant?

Max looks out the window at the fireworks. Waits for a flash, knowing the bang will follow. Keeping his own .45 on Lenny, he aims Lenny's Glock at the catatonic Gant.
BLAM! One right into Philo's forehead. The crack of thunder from the fireworks masks the sound.

MAX

You just did.

LENNY

Jesus!

MAX

You know, statistically that's the second most common word people say right before they die. *Shit* being number one.

Max sticks Lenny's Glock in his waistband, keeping his own .45 trained on Lenny.

LENNY

So . . . I killed Gant, then you ran in, being on his payroll, and shot me.

MAX

That's pretty much the way it happened.

CUT TO FAITH in the living room, moving silently up to the edge of the doorframe. She looks through the crack between the door and the jam. Her POV: Max with the gun on Lenny.

LENNY

Wait a minute. Now I'm remembering. I killed Iris too, didn't I?

MAX

That's right. They'll find the snuff tape at your apartment. The original. The one I left at the club for you was a copy.

LENNY

Was I a really busy guy? Did I do Tran too?

MAX

No. Those two whacko cops musta taken care a that for you. Saved you a stop.

Lenny drops the cutesy role.

LENNY

So why Max . . . why didya have to do Iris? She never hurt anybody.

CU FAITH, reacting to this.

MAX

Picture it . . . I feel I gotta share this with some-body. It's too perfect.

LENNY

I won't say anything.

MAX

I know. So picture it . . . I'm working for this puke, right? And he says he'll pay me quite large to do the hooker, but also I gotta do his bitch girlfriend because she's totally out of control. Only he doesn't know about me and Faith. So I say to myself, if I turn the job down, he just gets somebody else. And I lose Faith . . . to coin a phrase. So I tell him sure, why not, but I can't just cap your girlfriend pal, she's too well known, we gotta set up a chump. And who better than her loser ex-boyfriend, a known criminal, who's been seen harassing her in public many times.

LENNY

And who was, regrettably, also your <u>best fucking friend!</u>

MAX

No plan is perfect, Lenny.

LENNY

So you must be so pleased. I followed your jelly-bean trail right here, like a good little chump.

MAX

You got froggy on me a couple times. But I thought that riff about the Death Squad and all that con-

spiracy paranoia was pretty good. I hadda keep
you from bringing cops into it.

LENNY

So it was just those two loose cannons running
around.

MAX

Yeah, covering their butts. Pretty zany, huh?
Cheer up, Lenny. World's gonna end in ten minutes anyway. Nothing means nothing. You know
that. It's all shit. Look around . . . the whole planet's in total fucking chaos. You gotta take what you
can, while you can. 'Cause some shitbird can come
up and put a fuckin .22 in the back a your head any
second. Jeez, am I ranting again? Gotta watch that.

LENNY

How did you hook up with Faith?

MAX

This bonehead hires me a month ago to eyeball
her, right? But Faith knows me from you, right, so
she comes up to me and says, hey, Max, why you
following me and I say, I'll buy you a drink and
explain, and she says . . .

FAITH

So, do you enjoy watching me?

Max turns and sees her in the doorway.

MAX

You were supposed to go downstairs, baby.

FAITH

I know. I don't always do exactly what I'm told. So

I said, do you enjoy watching me? And you said—
come on, Max—

MAX
I said, yeah. I'd even do it for free.

FAITH
Uh huh. And I said, that's good, because I like the
feeling of someone watching me. I acquired the
taste from Lenny.

Lenny looks between Faith and Max, feeling like the asshole
of the western world. Faith moves up close to Max. She puts
her hands lightly on his shoulders, caressing them.
Max grins, realizing she is 100 percent with him.

MAX
(to Lenny) And then she said since we're going to
be spending so much time together—

FAITH
We might as well make the best of it.

Faith runs her hands appreciatively over Max's shoulders
and arms.
Then, in an eyeblink, she grabs his forearm in both hands
and deflects the gun.

FAITH
Lenny!!

Lenny jumps in, wrestling Max for the gun.
Faith pulls the Glock out of Max's waistband and throws it
across the room.

MAX

<u>Fucking bitch!!</u>

BLAM! BLAM! Max fires wildly, trying to hit Lenny, who
is just barely keeping the muzzle out of his face.
Faith grabs Max's hair, trying to pull him away . . .
His "hair" comes off in her hands. A prosthetic wig, contain-
ing the squid-net array.
Max's head is shaved to a Sinead O'Connor stubble.
He looks demonic, grimacing with effort as he struggles with
Lenny.
He continues firing . . .
The shots hit the mirrors. ANGLES of the reflected images
of them shattering. Faith, screaming, reflected . . . her face
fragmenting into shards.

Max is stronger and heavier than Lenny, but Lenny has one
advantage:
Max has managed to make him really, really angry.
Lenny gives a guttural cry and drives Max backward, slamming him into the doorframe. They tumble together into the
living room, falling together over the couch. Lenny pounds
Max's hands against the glass coffee table, shattering it. He
forces Max's hand along a glass edge, cutting it, and Max
drops the gun. Lenny reaches for it, but Max kicks it away
a split-second before his hand touches it.
It skitters under the couch, out of play.
He punches Lenny brutally in the face, then in the gut, and
grabs him with both hands. He hurls him against the wall.
Lenny staggers off the wall into several vicious punches
from Max.
We feel the tide turning. Lenny goes down to one knee.
Max pulls out his knife and flicks it open.
Lenny throws a lamp.
Max ducks and charges through.
Lenny spins away from the downthrust.

The knife imbeds itself in his shoulder blade, sunk in to the bone.
Lenny punches Max in the throat and jerks away, pulling the knife handle out of Max's hand.

Max tackles him and they crash together through a sliding glass door onto the balcony. Explosion of flying glass.

Max pulls a dazed Lenny to his feet and rushes him backward toward the railing. At the last instant, Lenny twists with all his strength and spins Max into the railing, using his weight against him.
He pushes hard and Max topples.

As he is going over, Max grabs Lenny's tie, pulling him over. Max is dangling 12 stories above the oblivious crowd, his entire weight hanging from Lenny's tie.
Lenny has one arm and one foot hooked around the railing, and he is being strangled by the tie.
Lenny is starting to black out.
In agony he gropes with his free hand to his own shoulder blade, finding the handle of the knife. He jerks it out of himself.
Max sees it coming a split second before it happens.
Lenny slashes the knife across the tie, just above Max's hands.
Max takes the express elevator to Hell.
He hits 12 stories down, on top of a video truck.

Lenny stands there panting, bleeding down the back of his jacket.
Faith runs to the railing and looks down.
All the strength goes out of her legs. She sags to the floor, her face crumpling in tears. She begins a hopeless, lost, keening sound.
Fireworks continue to boom across the sky.

Lenny looks down at her, gazing at the object of his quest. She looks up at him, her wet eyes seemingly at the bottom of a deep well from which he cannot save her.
He turns and walks away.

DOWN BELOW, in the madness of the crowd, we move with Steckler as he searches for Mace. He sees her from behind, walking near one of the stages. He moves up behind her, aiming his pistol at the back of her head. She turns and—
It isn't Mace. Another girl in a similar dress.
Steckler curses and looks around.

Engelman catches a glimpse of Mace running. He points to her position and Steckler charges after her. He has his baton laid back along his forearm and is clubbing people out of the way as he runs.

Mace kicks off her high heels and sprints barefoot through the crowd, pushing people out of her way. Strobe-lights from the stage and flashes from the fireworks give the crowd a nightmarish look.
Steckler fires at her. People drop, their screams drowned out by the pandemonium. The gunshots don't register above the concussions from the fireworks. No one notices the shootings.
Steckler continues to fire, missing her as people block his shots.
Mace won't fire back in the crowd.

ON STECKLER, coming to a stop at the base of a lighting tower.
He has lost sight of her. He starts to reload his pistol.
Mace comes up to him silently from behind the tower and hammer punches him behind the ear with the butt of her pistol.
Steckler comes around with a roar, slamming the baton

across her forearm. Her .380 clatters to the ground. Mace bodyslams him back against the steel tower, smashing her palm up under his chin. His head raps off the metal.

Mace is like a she-panther.

She rips the baton out of his hands and cracks him once across the windpipe. He drops to his knees, gagging and unable to breathe.

A shot hits the metal space-frame next to her head. She spins to see Engelman, charging toward her. Before he can fire again she drops behind the kneeling, gasping Steckler, using him as a human wall.

She clamps an arm around his neck, controlling him, and pulls his tazer from his belt. She shoots Engelman in the chest from 8 feet.

He convulses and drops instantly to the pavement, flopping like a fish. She holds the current on him while she goes over and kicks his gun away.

She takes Engelman's cuffs from his belt. Steckler glares at her through the blood running into his eyes. She raises the baton.

MACE
All the way down! RIGHT NOW!!

He slowly drops to the pavement, face-down. Now that she's got them both proned out, she quickly handcuffs one of Steckler's hands to one of Engelman's.

The crowd of partiers stares. Can't believe what they're seeing.

Mace takes Steckler's cuffs and attaches his other wrist to the base of the tower. That's when THREE LAPD COPS in riot gear burst through the surrounding crowd and see a black girl crouching over two of LA's finest with a police baton. The cops advance toward her.

MACE
Wait. Let me tell you what's going on here—

The nearest shoots her with a tazer.
She spasms and goes to her hands and knees.
One of the cops kicks her down.
She cries out, trying to explain, but she can't get the breath
as the batons start to fall.
The crowd around them watches fascinated, gaping.
Mace sees another cop arrive and start to uncuff Steckler.

MACE
NO!! NO!!!

They crack her with their batons, telling her to stay down.
Another one kicks her in the stomach.

A BLACK KID in the crowd leaps onto one of the kicking
cops.
And then they come out of the crowd . . . one, then three,
then half a dozen. Just normal people . . . black, white, Lat-
ino people . . . that can't watch this shit happen any more.
They jump the cops, swarming them, wrestling them down.
It becomes a brawl.
Then cops are running in from everywhere. We see the trig-
ger point of a full-scale riot. Cops in full riot-gear, with
Lexan shields, push the crowd back, clearing a space.
A helicopter XENON comes straight down from above, like
the divine light of God.

Mace hugs herself, at the center of it, unable to get up.
Within seconds there are 20 cops there, and more on the
way, forming a human wall. They get the crowd settled
down.
Through the phalanx of riot cops comes Palmer Strickland
and several ranking officers.

He surveys the scene. Strickland looks down at Mace and
then at Steckler and Engelman, who are getting to their
knees, though still handcuffed to each other and the steel
tower.

> **STRICKLAND**
> (to the nearest officers) These two are under ar-
> rest for murder.

Strickland looks Steckler in the eye and holds up Lenny's
squid tape.
Steckler and Engelman react, knowing they are over.

> **STRICKLAND**
> And get some medical attention for this woman.

The helicopter xenon gives the whole moment an other-
worldly quality. Like they are in some celestial court of judgment.

Lenny pushes through from behind Strickland. He runs to
Mace and kneels next to her.

> **LENNY**
> Are you okay?

She is still dazed. A trickle of blood runs down her face.
She nods weakly and reaches for him. They hug, then they
both wince in pain.
Mace sees the cops running in to arrest Steckler and En-
gelman.
One of them unhooks Steckler from the tower.

> **MACE**
> I got 'em, Lenny.

LENNY
Mace the ace. You're amazing.

Engelman lunges, grabbing a gun from the holster of the closest cop.
He waves them back with it.
Then puts it in his mouth and fires.
He topples against Steckler, spraying him with his spurting blood.
Steckler clutches him, lowering him to the ground, bathing in his blood.
You see him going insane, right at that moment.
His face is bloodstreaked and suddenly demonic.

Steckler, the street-monster cop, RISES IN SLOW MOTION.
His glare is fixed on Lenny and Mace. He has Engelman's gun in one blood-drenched hand.
Lifting the dead weight of Engelman by the handcuff, he begins to drag the body, lurching toward Mace. He keeps the pistol down along his side.
Steckler exists at the center of a circle of cops who don't know what to do. He has a gun so they can't rush him. But he's a cop, so they can't shoot him. Several officers are shouting at him to drop the weapon.
You barely hear them over the pandemonium of the crowd, the helicopter, the fireworks.

LENNY
SHOOT!!

Like a scene from a nightmare the blood-drenched Steckler, completely unhinged, lurches toward them. Engelman's body slides over the ground, leaving a snail-track of blood a foot wide.

SPREG
YOU FUCKING NIGGER BITCH!!

He raises Engelman's pistol and points it at her.
Lenny throws himself across her, turning his back to take
the fire.
POW POW POW!
The LAPD executes Steckler in a hail of fire.
He drops like a sack of cement.
Lenny realizes he is alive. He faints.
Mace shakes him, thinking he is shot. He opens his eyes.

LENNY
Yeah, what?

CUT TO SEVERAL MINUTES LATER. Mace and Lenny
are being escorted through the crowd by Strickland and a
number of cops. They are jostled and shoved by the rowdy
mob, who aren't paying any attention to the cops passing
through.
They pass DEATH, with the (plastic) BABY still in his arms.
Lenny pushes the scythe out of the way so they can get past.

MACE
Are we under arrest?

LENNY
Naw. They just have to ask us a few questions . . .
for about six hours.

MACE
Where's Faith?

LENNY
Faith who?

We pass the CLOCK MIME, who smiles at them and puts his hands at midnight. We hear a roar passing through the crowd. A huge chanting and cheering, that becomes thunderous.

Lenny and Mace look around . . . the wonder of it sinking in.

30 seconds till midnight. Until the beginning of the 21st century.

> **MACE**
> Looks like we made it, Lenny.

Lenny starts to grin. He taps Strickland on the shoulder and signals for him to stop. All around them people begin to shout the countdown to midnight.

> **CROWD**
> TEN! NINE! EIGHT! . . .

Lenny shouts with them.

> **LENNY (AND CROWD)**
> SEVEN! SIX! FIVE! . . .

Mace grins at him and starts to chant too.

> **MACE**
> FOUR! THREE! TWO! ONE! HAPPY NEW YEAR!!

The exultation of the moment flows through them as they lift their voices with the crowd in a great cheer. Balloons are released, confetti and streamers fly in a blizzard. Couples grab each other and kiss passionately. Lenny sees all these people around him kissing.

He and Mace look at each other. It floods through Lenny's
brain like a burst of fireworks. Nothing ever felt more right.
He grabs her and plants one on her like in the movies.
She grabs his head and won't let him break even if he
wanted to, which he doesn't.
Strickland rolls his eyes and waits. Looks at his watch.
Escorted by a couple of cops, Faith passes near them. She is
in handcuffs and her eyes are dull.
She sees Lenny and Mace, as she passes, but they don't see
her.

12:01 AM, January 1, 2000

PULL BACK AND UP as Lenny and Mace stay locked together, while the cops wait for them, and the world begins
again.

DUTTON   ℗ **PLUME**

GRIPPING SUSPENSE

☐ **THE LIGHTHOUSE AT THE END OF THE WORLD by Stephen Marlowe.** The year is 1849. Edgar Allan Poe, famous for his writing, infamous for his scandalous ways, has disappeared for much of a week before surfacing at a Baltimore hospital, mortally ill. What, in that blank space of time, has he done? Here is an extraordinary tour-de-force of narrative suspense, historical realism, and surreal enchantment, a novel that rivals its hero's greatest tales. "Imaginative . . . hovers daringly between fact and fiction."—Jay Parini   (940499—$23.95)

☐ **THE WITCHES' HAMMER by Jane Stanton Hitchcock.** A rich, complex, relentlessly suspenseful thriller which blends chilling evil that is at once centuries old and efficiently modern, and probes the dark paths of eroticism and madness. Beatrice O'Connell's orderly life is shattered when her father, a gentle man preoccupied with rare-book collecting, is viciously murdered.   (936416—$21.95)

☐ **NIGHT VISION by Ronald Munson.** A legend among hackers, Cyberwolf is a natural genius, a maverick, faster and better than any of the competition—prowling cyberspace, lurking in the electronic shadows. Now he has chosen Susan Bradstreet, one of Hollywood's reigning stars and, unluckily for her, Cyberwolf's object of desire as his target. Isolated in his grip, she schemes to save herself with all the cunning she can muster.   (937811—$21.95)

☐ **DOGS OF GOD by Pinckney Benedict.** The psychopathic Tannhauser, a backwoodsman turned drug lord, rules savagely in an abandoned resort in the West Virginia mountains that he has made an impregnable fortress. Into his realm comes Goody, an itinerant bare-knuckle fighter who is too proud to give in to ruthless power. The stage is set for an excursion into violence and an exploration of evil. "A stunning novel."—New York Times Book Review   (273706—$10.95)

☐ **BONE DEEP by Darian North.** In this harrowing suspense novel, a beautiful young forensic anthropologist delves into her own past to reveal shocking secrets that touch off deadly danger, until suddenly everything connects—sinew and flesh, heart and soul.   (938494—$23.95)

☐ **STRANGE DAYS Original text and Introduction by James Cameron.** Los Angeles, December 30, 1999. Through neon nights and strange days moves Lenny Nero, street hustler, ex-cop, and panhandler of stolen dreams. He sells "clips"—little bits of people's lives—everything they saw, heard, and felt for thirty minutes, captured on a digital recording. He can make anything happen. But when someone anonymously slips him the killer's clip of a brutal murder, Lenny can't help but become an emotional accomplice.   (275814—$12.95)

Prices slightly higher in Canada.

Visa and Mastercard holders can order Plume, Meridian, and Dutton books by calling
1-800-253-6476.
They are also available at your local bookstore. Allow 4-6 weeks for delivery.
This offer is subject to change without notice.

DUTTON

EXPLOSIVE THRILLERS

☐ **THE TAKEOVER by Stephen W. Frey.** This taut, high-speed thriller about the power and politics of money takes you into the world of investment banking. Andrew Falcon has staked his whole future on the biggest hostile takeover in Wall Street history, one that will net him a fee of $5 million—if he can pull it off fast. But soon he stumbles upon a secret scheme behind the takeover . . . a plot so vast and brilliantly designed as to stagger the imagination. "Absolutely first-rate . . . a fast moving plot in the Ludlum tradition."—James Patterson, author of *Kiss the Girls* (939857—$19.95)

☐ **YOU CAN'T CATCH ME by Rosamond Smith.** This novel is a spellbinding work of riveting psychological suspense by a literary virtuoso. It is a story in which no one is who they seem and where murderous rage lurks behind every exquisite façade. The moment genteel Southern bachelor Tristram Heade arrives in Philadelphia he is mistaken everywhere for a man of whom he has never heard but soon comes to know fearfully well. (939474—$19.95)

☐ **KARMA by Mitchell Smith.** A riveting thriller that blends complex emotion with nail-biting suspense. A powerful exploration of greed, forbidden love, and betrayal. In a world destined by fate, there are moments that are beyond any one person's control. For Evan Scott, that moment comes when he witnesses a woman plunging thirty stories to her death. (937730—$22.95)

☐ **FLAWLESS by Adam Barrow.** The dark heart of a serial killer is at the center of this powerful thriller of death and redemption. Michael Woodrow is a flawlessly handsome and intelligent 30-year-old. As successful as he is as a corporate consultant, he cannot control his compulsion to kill. And kill again. His father, Norman, is every inch the educated English professor of distinction. Now in his sixties, he's finally been released from jail. (940472—$22.95)

Prices slightly higher in Canada.

Visa and Mastercard holders can order Plume, Meridian, and Dutton books by calling
1-800-253-6476.
They are also available at your local bookstore. Allow 4-6 weeks for delivery.
This offer is subject to change without notice.

DUTTON Ⓟ **PLUME**

CAPTIVATING NOVELS

☐ **TOO DAMN RICH by Judith Gould.** At the heart of this mesmerizing novel are three vibrant women, each as stunningly beautiful as they are dangerously ambitious, caught up in a glittering world of wealth, power, and passion. The action revolves around Burghley's, the oldest, most venerated and respected auction house in the world. It has become a seething hotbed of ravenous greed and intricate intrigue for those whose prestige is nourished by what—and who—they possess.   (936653—$24.95)

☐ **PLAYLAND by John Gregory Dunne.** The search for the answer to the tantalizing question—of what happened to Blue Tyler, the adorable child star who grew up to be an exquisite sexpot—sends cynical screenwriter Jack Broderick on a probe through movieland's golden past and gilded guilts in a wide-screen saga of lust, greed, violence, ambition, secrets, and even a touch of true love that gives the reader a feast of show-and-tell, and brings a dazzling array of fantasyland characters to life. "A complex novel about power, fame, lust and murder. . . . Dunne's best book."—*Boston Globe*   (274958—$13.95)

☐ **THE LOOK by Nina Blanchard.** This is a novel about the head of a modeling agency, Jessica Cartwright, and her greatest discovery, Caddie Dean, who has risen from a past she desperately wants to keep hidden to the very top of the modeling pyramid. Their dreams all seem to have come true—until the handsome, brutally ambitious man Caddie has married sets out to use her as his ticket to success. It exposes the ambitions, cruelty, and seductions of those who feed fashion's voracious appetite for fame, power, and money.   (937951—$23.95)

☐ **MILLIONAIRES ROW by Norman Katkov.** A scorching novel of murder, ambition, seduction and justice in the heart of the Deep South. North Carolina in 1932 is the domain of the all-powerful Castleton dynasty. When 22-year-old Kyle Castleton, heir to the family fortune, is found shot to death in his bedroom, the Castletons swiftly change the official cause of death from suicide to murder. Two suspects are fingered: Faith Castleton, Kyle's stunning young wife and a star of the Broadway stage, and Boyd Fredericks, a "townee" who was Kyle's boyhood friend.   (938435—$23.95)

☐ **SPECIAL RELATIONSHIP by Robyn Sisman.** An extraordinary novel that has all the passion and immediacy of today's headlines. Sweeping from the wild student scene of Oxford in the sixties to the cutthroat political arena of the present, this story measures the explosive ramifications of a secret, twenty-year-old love affair between a lovely Englishwoman and the charismatic American running for the presidency.   (938729—$22.95)

Prices slightly higher in Canada.